Dear Great-Grandson

By Christopher Waddington

Published by the author:

Morley House	Waimarama Rd
Little Silver	R.D. Rakaia
Muddiford	Canterbury
North Devon	New Zealand
EX31 4HQ	
UK	

Cover illustration by Great-Grandfather
Edited by Bradstock & Associates, Christchurch, New Zealand
Designed and printed by Microfilm Digital Print, Christchurch, New Zealand

ISBN 978-0-473-14558-3

Author's preface

Dear Great-Grandson arose from the author's sense of duty to relate to descendants details of a fraud on their forbear's estate. Mindful that a reader's tolerance for complexity has its limits in such matters, I have restricted explanations to one-tenth of the book. I hope this aspect will amount to a cautionary tale. The rest concerns my own and ancestors' lives which I am confident are most unusual. They concern business ventures that in retrospect seem scarcely credible. Relief from this turmoil is provided by alarming adventures with an old ketch. Curiosity concerning the sea more than satisfied, he is glad to return to reap the bounty of the land. The narrative is in letter form without chapters:

- Introduction

- Discovery of Grandfather's family portrait

- Grandfather's anxious, even terrified appearance in a family portrait

- Anxiety as both illness and motivator

- Grandfather's son (in portrait), emigrates to New Zealand for a short period and returns

- Marries in England and in 1940 sends wife and son to New Zealand on pretext of the war

- His wife's struggle without connection or referral to anyone in that country

- Auckland in the 1940s and 50s

- A notorious convent school – then the posh preparatory

- University, waterfront work and strikes; the 'wool boom'

- Son leaves in hope of a career in haute couture

- Four weeks shipboard; the rectitude of sheep farmers' wives

- Meeting with father aged 20, and its effects

- Living in London and Paris

- Work in Paris; the atmosphere and de Gaulle's return to power

- Father's new young wife and the business synergies of their union

- Son's failure in haute couture and at all levels of the rag trade

- The fraud

- Adventures sailing an old ketch in the Atlantic and Mediterranean

- Conclusion: life on the land.

Christopher Waddington
North Devon, 2008

Dear Great-Grandson,

This letter, addressed to you with some embarrassment, is redeemed in part in that respect because your great-grandfather had no initial desire to reach a wider public. This is a personal letter and so you may be better able to forgive shortcomings in this narrative with events and descriptions that at times seem unremarkable. Yet the distance between us of three generations provides interest in itself, assisted, of course, by the fact that, terrestrially at least, we are unlikely to meet! My forbears, five generations distant, in common with their neighbours did not travel beyond 16 miles of their homes, in many cases, throughout their whole lives. Thirty-two miles for horse and rider to ensure safe return before nightfall was the limit for the family mount. Facts such as these illustrate change.

But beyond those lives of our distant kin are the folk of both your time and mine. So your great-grandfather hopes to hold your interest as he knows your father well. Grandchildren are an aging life's compensation. They bring joy which at times their care-worn parents can barely fathom. Of course it is this pleasure that has prompted your great-grandfather to write to you.

Often sons are stern judges of their fathers, and so only after this attempt was well advanced did I tell your grandfather of it.

Dad: "I'm writing a book."

Son: "Oh."

Later:

Dad: "As I told you the book ... you know ... it's a monograph in so far as it treats of one subject: great-grandfatherhood. Or perhaps it's a family history, although one of the family said pointedly to me, "What do *you* know about the family?" I hesitate to call it an autobiography as that genre is generally reserved for people of achievement, and we needn't go into that."

Son: "No."

Dad: "And on that subject, I believe that the autobiography *Diary of a Nobody* is largely an intentional sting on the reader by the author. The reader is the snob as he is led by the nose to belittle Pooter. Most readers would fail to see that they share Pooter's pretensions and insignificance."

Son: "You are too defensive: don't let it worry you ... and anyway I've never heard of this Mr Nobody."

Much later:

Dad: "This book … I'll never finish it … I'll *die* before I finish it."

Son: "I sympathise. I can't find the time for reading either."

Dad: "No! No! The one I'm *writing*! Not *reading*!"

Son: "Oh."

Later again:

Dad: "The book … I've had a terrible thought. I won't be *allowed* to die until I've finished it, and anyway no-one'll read it."

Son: "Well all right, finish it, I'll read it. But keep it short and humorous."

But, dear Great-Grandson, this account cannot be just light and entertaining, because it concerns the necessity to describe a fraud. My hope is that you may draw lessons from it even if you feel that Great-grandfather was too gullible. After all, it is natural for a parent to hope to be of use – anxious that his descendants will have achievements beyond his own.

Beware the person with the permanent rictus of a smile. Generally, those that create, administer and apply the law are more tolerant of white-collar crime yet profess forever that they are not. This observation is so commonplace that your great-grandfather is embarrassed to recount what you may already know. A burglar might take your money and may be caught and locked up. Whereas a crooked lawyer (who together with all of his profession is also designated an 'Officer of the Court' in order to see justice reign), will *take* your money, make you *pay* while he takes your money, and make you *wait* while he takes your money until you have no money left.

But even this may not be the limit of his success. He might frame *you* as the culprit who obstructed other beneficiaries to a will from obtaining what is rightfully theirs while running the estate clean out of funds – funds he uses for his own benefit. Thus inculpated, the odium you now bear might last beyond a generation. Of course he will, too, have the skill to suggest that *you* are the author of your own misfortunes, and even conspire with others to fatten your fee-paying file and paint you as the vexatious litigant.

To this end he will even write letters to himself, in the guise of writing to third parties with information they do not need, or if they do likely already have. Yes, his professional body will on complaint 'tax' i.e. eliminate such correspondence from charge – but at what point in the proceedings? Obviously, in practice, only after rupture, when the damage is done and all confidence is lost is a reckoning demanded. Bear in mind too that until his account is settled, the file remains your lawyer's property.

Dear Great-Grandson, the best field for the play described concerns inheritance. Opportunity presents itself to the unscrupulous because no testator can intervene from beyond the grave. Expanding upon this theme, Charles Dickens wrote *Bleak House* which one literary notable described as one of the six greatest novels in the language. In this work Dickens saw no need to treat of a single fact or issue in dispute. It was enough to his purpose to portray the law's delays as so corrosive that ever-increasing expectation takes a young beneficiary to an early grave. Then with leaden irony the lawyers exult that, to the honour of their profession, they have seen justice done: the money for their efforts is exhausted at last and they are beyond reproach.

Finally your great-grandfather must refer to the religious influence of his very early years that instilled an uncompromising view towards wrongdoing. For one of tender years this had much force ('Give me a child before the age of ten and I'll give you the man,' says the Jesuit.) One was strictly taught the precept that 'crime does not pay' in reference to accountability in the life hereafter, and vividly reminded of the inevitable meeting with Saint Peter at the gate. Yet later one then encountered seemingly excellent people whose view of theft (graced as it might be by the word 'fraud') was more than equivocal: 'Just don't get caught.'

One tenth only of what follows concerns fraud (and sadly must include some facts). Then as a further self-indulgence there is a page or two on political meddlings in private property. The rest, strictly to your own grandfather's instructions, is lighter.

All in all the writer is relieved to be quit of a duty whether or not the account is heeded – or indeed read.

He woke, startled by the unfamiliar place. Ah, yes: his young son's newly rented house. Not a frequent visitor – the objects are still strange. But what's this? A formal portrait arranged with solemn dignity for a special occasion in an Edwardian family. And what a contrast with portraits since! Now the hope is that casualness will impart significance through a fleeting moment while their inevitable photographic fate is to drown with their like, discarded and awash in drawers. Not here! Mother, father and their eight children are posed in their best, and the intention to project their natures is in every way achieved. Slow film exposure and the serious occasion both forbade a frozen smile to excellent and serious effect.

The mother, conscious of her added status conferred through her children, is attentive yet relaxed. The father? Set to run a mile! Even the stillness of the formal occasion fails to mask his anxiety. This very first encounter now, in his son's strange house sees the grandson overjoyed to make the acquaintance of his grandfather and soulmate.

Elated by the discovery, the visitor dresses quickly and rushes from the house. Once he is free in the street an enhanced sense of self-identity descends in his 64th year. So much less now of 'Who is he? Where does he come from?' – unremarkable though that may be in these times of fractured families. An added happy dimension too: his own son had, quite unprompted, framed and placed this portrait of his own great-grandfather and family. The visitor, knowing little of his own father, had identified him at once. Among eight siblings there is no mistaking him, for as he is the second youngest, his rival brother is swaddled on his mother's lap.

Years earlier the visitor had heard he was born on his grandfather's birthday in 1937 – also the year of his death. Should these coincidences continue, with his grandfather's death aged 68, his grandson has four years to live, until 2004. Perhaps there is time to celebrate this happy meeting with the gentleman on tenterhooks as he peers anxiously from the picture frame.

This subject's own father went north to Scotland from Yorkshire in about 1860. As a law clerk aged 19 he became an excise man imposing whisky duty at Fettercairn, near Stonehaven. He married a local farmer's daughter and later took his young family to the Hebrides with the Customs Service. This meant that the first language of the father in the portrait was Gaelic.

The subject's own father may possibly have gone north because he was illegitimate. No record of his birth has been found in the Parish register although all other members of the Bradford family are recorded, including a male lodger at the same address. The subject's own father had, however, been recorded in the 1851 census. Had he been brought up as a brother whilst his real mother was in fact his sister?

Great-grandfather was then sent south with his family to Tunbridge Wells in Kent. So the brandy smugglers of the English Channel became his quarry rather than the illicit whisky stills of the not-long-subdued Scottish Highlands. These were chaotic times following Napoleon III's defeat at Sedan. With the anarchy of the Paris Commune, France was in disorder. Smugglers and excisemen were armed, with skirmishes a common event.

The exciseman's son must have made a fair fist of his second language, English, as he went on to teach Classics as a schoolmaster. He then went into business, including farming, which he followed with mixed success before jumping with his family into the portrait somewhere along the way.

Orphans, semi-orphans and the like are best placed to perceive the mystique of family. These, especially when young, peering in from without see the family as a homogeneous entity. Conversely, family members see themselves first as individuals and family members second. The new outsider sees the whole wood before he sees each tree. Some family-children cleave to its ideals and sentiments, and therefore for them its life-sustaining memories. These are the loyal members of the family's body politic. Other siblings recall only their worst experiences and the family's constraints.

To go into a strange family to live is a huge event for an only child. Sophisticated notions of 'alternatives' or whether his situation is 'inevitable' are not in his consciousness. Nor are there 'expectations': there are only the events of life as it unfolds. Once through the family's door he will never escape his 'observer' status as the one from the outside observing those on the inside. The child might for safety or from embarrassment wish himself between the wall and the wallpaper, and believe too he has effaced himself; and all to no avail: his presence is noted for as long as he is with them. The analogy with this description is that as a child in the family portrait, of those who are in it, there may be some who are less so, and then outside the frame is the observer who, though he may live among them, can never be in the frame at all.

The portrait's second-youngest left early for farm work overseas. In sentiment he may have been estranged from his family. To two separate women he confided later that he never recovered from losing the attentions of his mother and siblings which he had enjoyed until the arrival of her last child. His decision to emigrate was no doubt influenced by the Great War. This had claimed the lives of so many teachers that all education suffered. He did not welcome inquiries about the past. Of the two types of family siblings he was of the less nostalgic persuasion. Although not bluff in manner, his advice in face of the vagaries of life was "Get on or get out!" In judgment of a man's work his verdict might be "Twenty years' worth of one year's experience!" A stiff-backed 'what-you-see-is-all-you-need-to-know' attitude was usual with the conformities of the times. People did not unbend and explain themselves: to do so would have been thought a sign of weakness and insecurity.

These first outlines in a character-portrait of this son, with what is known further, make plain that the chronic anxiety of the father in the photo-portrait had been passed to his son completely. This is not just anxiety that can be motivating in life, but rather the anxiety that is a hair's breadth from panic. The impact of this affliction is not lessened, though it be shared by so many and passed onwards.

The Oregon

On the plain
in the throat of the gorge
the wind increases.
Sweeping from mountains
this commonplace event
Of little moment
to those long settled
Though more
to all disposed
to fear the worst
They hark to each new shriek,
of this wind's howling pitch
Shrunk beneath their roofs,
afrighted in the fields.
As branches strew the land –
the fallen in the fight
The cattle lower droop their heads
on their feet, and in the lee,
But windward of this herd
some sentinels do stand
Deployed in single line abreast
the Oregon ...(the Douglas fir)
They're keen to greet this wind with valour
and stream their bannered tresses out
Raked branches like pagoda'd roofs
dressed round, to each its own design.
They dip, rise, swing, sway
to leeward, then return
And parry each and every thrust
the wind no quarter given

Their sombre green
in emerald flush
With golden cones heaped feathery soft,
the treasure that befits theme
Yet still the Gods must rage,
upon this thin green line
Till comes a pause,
a sea-shell sound
of millions pressed to ear.
The dreaded wind increases yet
with the sound of surfing seas
Yet the trees, our shore,
will break its back
we know they'll never yield.

C.S. Waddington

Now the gale has fled these trees, the gracious, adornments of the field – their company offered to man and beast. For the solitary man at work, introspection and the self-importance engendered by solitude may be given unfettered attention: hermitry, said the sage, is indulgence in the self. There is, too, a feeling of competence, even illusions of power that stream from simple toil. The heavy hoe is swung high then down, for the trees must greet some new recruits to face the hated wind. The introvert, jealous in his domain, is glad to see no rival. The sheep and cattle are deferential in their attention. With each day spent in three equal parts – grazing, social life and sleep – they have leisure to watch the propping, stooping biped in their midst. Exchange of gaze, man to beast, enhances comprehension to mutual benefit. Better still, the man is the centre of attention.

Yet with time, changes of weather, light or simply fits of caprice, a curmudgeonly defensiveness might descend to replace this self-esteem. Grievances are then explored and expanded: this is manual work: healthy for the body, sometimes less so for the mind. But there is a nervous smile for others and he hopes not just for those who are seldom met. As with an agoraphobic in his house, this is a haven from fear and anxiety. It is a refuge from that part of life that is just somehow lived. These precisely tonsured fields where form follows function have yet an honest charm in their strict utility. The indifferent townsman should reconsider as his eye sweeps the view. Shining grass, trees, mountains and sky combine together in a scene unrivalled anywhere. Ambling stock and racing cloud lend movement to the picture beyond a painter's compass. Full-billowed clouds on ships of light run downwind, throwing shadows as they please upon the fields beneath. Such clouds defy capture. The artist must turn to the mountains: they won't sail away. As to the locals, they just look at them for the weather.

Grandfather's son emigrating in the twenties viewed the scene differently. "'Cows?" he said. "If I had to do *that* again they'd be milking themselves!" As a successful inventor in later life such a comment could not be ignored. One heard he had to work so hard for his farming masters that he took to the road as a salesman. No details of his early life were offered. Probably only women were privy to his experiences and innermost thoughts. His last confided that just days before he died in Florida the scent of new-mown hay brought back the memory of how hard he had had to work. Although not quite of the type known as a ladies' man who often despise male company, one doubts he confided in men. To do so would have conveyed a lack of self-confidence. Women, apart from their natural allure, needed protection and attention – not an uncommon notion in the early twentieth century when many men thought of women as of another species.

This is the story of an Edwardian family portrait and an attempt to describe the fear in the father as he peers from the frame. The shock to the grandson was greater for seeing the photograph for the first time in his own son's house. He was compelled to explain what he had seen.

Grandfather's son was so guarded and restrained, he proffered few observations. But one was salutary: "We could not be like that: there is too much anxiety in family." His own son's eyes opened wide at this because as with his own father, he also knew nothing of his forbears. The son came to see that the de-motivating effect of fear and anxiety is an endless curse and can leave its victim as frozen as a rabbit bailed up by a ferret.

This son sublimated his fear each business morning with prolonged verbal attacks on selected subordinates. Though not aggressive physically, he had few equals in the techniques of damning reproach. Fear of failure rather than a desire for success motivated him entirely. Fortunately he did not seem to derive satisfaction from humiliating others. The victims at least were left in no doubt that the tirade was for their own good. Naturally this did not make them any happier, as he skilfully convinced them they were much at fault. The exercise did relieve his anxiety on a temporary basis – usually until the next morning. Employees might be dismissed and then re-appointed by his secretary with profuse apologies after they had stepped into the street. His fears were momentarily placated by these encounters as people were used to relieve his burden. He was most adept at reassuring victims that he was only trying to 'help' them. He drank little as it was said his own father did so to excess: nicotine from chain-smoking and caffeine from endless tea-drinking gave him the stimulus he needed.

His success so grimly won soon wore a different face owing to the 'do-your-own-thing' legacy of the sixties. Personal job satisfaction became an individual's basic requirement. Successful men and women now beamed from the business pages to show that it could all be such fun. As a pre-sixties London businessman he, like his peers, would have had a dignified notion of his hard-earned place in life. Memorably, he used to say, "I and men better than me think ..." This was an attitude of another time. His socially severe manner was a hindrance. When he entered a room, for some indefinable reason all conversation would cease. An uneasy dignity made him appear intimidating. When the party regained its composure his views and their delivery seemed declamatory and stilted. A man of firm convictions, one of his recurring themes was that women in marriage had too much security.

Yet with the dismantling of conformity in the sixties, although his manner could not change, he readily embraced the startling social changes of the time. His son was amazed at this about-face, and doubted his father's sincerity. Having had a big dose of the man's discipline hitherto, he was now the one to appear reactionary.

Milestones in Grandfather's son's early life are few. In a letter sent in 1928 his mother wrote that the Royal Mail steamer had been sighted off Start Point so she had hastened to catch the post before it turned round. Return voyages of more than four months would accentuate the isolation of any new immigrant. Unanswered questions due to letters being 'crossed in the post' through mishap or tardiness defeated any dialogue. Each corresponding party would thus be confined to a simple exchange of news. And so the process of assimilation became imperative: the settler must perforce assume the identity of his new land. He could not just flit between the two hemispheres at will. Rather he well might wallow in an eight-berth for eight weeks in the bowels of the RMS *Largs Bay*.

An undiscovered world beyond the confines of a farmer's boundary will tempt an agile mind. Grandfather's son was soon in business, although he never divulged its nature (and questions were discouraged). In his early thirties he returned (and this he did confide) to England to gain business experience. A young American tycoon named Frank Woolworth had revolutionised popular retail shopping. On finding work in Woolworth's stores the son became their youngest manager, at Bow in London. He insisted, he said, on promotion at every opportunity. The Sainsbury family were his next employers. They too were about to revolutionise their own field – the grocery trade – leading to the first supermarkets. In 2000 the second generation of this family lost its last member, well into his nineties. The firm's recruit recalled the family's furious business rows which, he said, so often indicated intense and therefore successful business commitment. Such stress had little effect on the health of Sainsbury's nonagenarian, as he outlived the new employee by more than 30 years.

The young man demonstrated his inventiveness with a prototype cash-register. "Now show me the bell that rings when the thief puts his hand in the till," said Mr Sainsbury. A colleague left a record of the occasion in a sketch. As to the thieves, the son had charge of some country boys lodged in the staff's hostel. One lad was caught with a chest full of half-crowns under his bed and provided no explanation other than "There was so much money I thought there could be no harm in having some." The son felt he could not punish such innocent ingenuousness, so the boy kept his job. Before long the boys in the son's charge were known as his 'forty thieves' – a case of loyalty bought with leniency.

He then found a post in an industry just beginning – as a management consultant. In 1935 he married and in 1937 his only child, a son, was born. The couple went to the Olympics at Berlin in 1936 and winter sports (as they were known). A new drophead Armstrong Siddley car and a contemporary art deco flat gave them style. Later, a new small mock Tudor house set in a Surrey pine wood was their home.

The tall sides of the lanes in that Surrey country are crowned with towering beeches. They and their ancestors have held these walls for centuries while at their feet the solid wagon wheels of the iron trade cut the lane ever deeper. Bullocks drew wagons of local ore, wood for charcoal and pig iron in all weathers. Many lanes were so deep (and dark) the crowning massive beeches only began their climb from above a man's height. Sent to fetch milk, the boy was terrified.

Nature here has with time forgiven then enhanced the imprint of man's past. Water-wheels drove hammers pounding iron in mill-houses built tight to ponds (also known as hammers). Gas-poisoned urchins dragged turfs from charcoal ovens. Red bricks ever baking built smelters ever smelting. Hissing steam or iron saw its quenching. Smoke, mud, rags, hovels, noise, and misery. How did nature triumph? Now autumn's red leaves drift across the water to blend with the bricks of silent barns.

Strange destination; a yet stranger time to travel. August 1940 found mother and child sailing down the English Channel. This event, much against the young wife's will and that of her family, was accepted on the assurance that she would be reunited with her husband "when this [war] is over". The *Tuscan Star*, a modern motor ship, was capable of good speed. With U-boats playing havoc, to be impeded by the oldest and slowest in the convoy moving at uniform pace would be a trial to any master. In the previous December the ship had been attacked from the air in the Channel. Through skilful swerving the captain had escaped with only one casualty. Now the convoy stolidly made its way; the occasional fiery glow on the horizon as a tanker blazed did not worry the child: for him it was just dawn or sunset on the sea. Disembarked in Panama for the ship's passage through the locks, they were obliged to hire a taxi. The driver refused to accept sterling in payment, for the invasion of Britain was thought imminent and her defeat certain. Eventually he accepted the money "to keep as a souvenir".

At journey's end a weekly paper showed a beautiful woman of 27 holding her boy of 3 1/2. The caption ungraciously if unintentionally described them as 'refugees'. Even 'evacuees' would have been wide of the mark as they had both been sent by her husband, passage-paid to guarantee their swift dispatch. (Two years later in September 1942 the *Tuscan Star* was torpedoed almost on the Equator, off the West African coast. Carrying a full cargo of frozen meat from the Argentine, she sank in three minutes. Captain Roberts skilfully evacuated all except two the company into the ship's boats. They waited until dawn in the hope that they might be found. Instead the U-boat appeared and took their radio operator captive, following which the rest all reached the coast and safety.)

On landing, there was a pressing need for the young woman to find work. Her husband had advised her to travel north to the largest city. As a family man he benefited from the married man's tax allowance, but remitted to his wife less than the difference he would have paid as a bachelor. Ever dutiful yet proud, but financially naive, the young woman neither complained nor sought redress. The banishment of wife and child, in dangerous circumstances, was in every way a boon for Grandfather's son.

Without introductions, connections or relations she set forth. How could such a woman – or indeed any person so fearless, impossible to aggravate or provoke: qualities that denote self-confidence – be yet so passive? After all, she could motivate herself in a near-crisis. She was in one now: travelling to a strange city in a small, young country with predictably insular attitudes rather than a tolerance for individual anonymity. Board and lodging had to be found when a young woman with a child knocking at any door in those days was looked at askance. She needed proximity to a kindergarten (a near-impossibility), and a kind landlady prepared to accept the child until the mother returned from work. Work? If work was available.

Her ability to cope in extremity fell well short of notions of self-interest or ambition. They were not in her armoury. Calmly she glided on with restrained poise and unflappable, detached, maddening serenity. Fittingly, this character was evident in her features. Too square a jaw was balanced with widely set blue eyes which enhanced her composure. Indeed they were so widely set that her features could not be read just at a glance.

Mother and son saw a city which compared with others in the world has a type of location unique to itself. It was founded on a narrow isthmus between two harbours. This locality remains its centre and heart. With respect to its current land area, it has spread to become the largest in the southern hemisphere. Attached to a small isolated country, its population growth was naturally curtailed although this allowed its citizens to live much as they chose, in comfortable bungalows with considerable gardens. The newcomers discovered a city with a population one-sixth what it is today.

Despite hardship there were compensations – some captivating, too! Sunny weather, taken for granted at any time of the year. But very determined rain, when that was scheduled. Several isolated green hills rose above its own personal sea of red roofs. They learned with surprise that these were extinct volcanoes. Genuinely golden beaches and a sparkling sea both close to hand conspired to make things tolerable no matter what.

Taking things for granted as those born to a place tend to do, one suspects that they were unaware of the reasons for their city's grandeur. With an ocean to the north and east, a sea to the west and neither more than 50 miles distant, the city's situation is unique. Wind from any direction brings moisture. Striking the heat of the land relative to the sea, the wind's moisture, suddenly heated, rushes up in ever-expanding, billowing clouds of vapour lit by the sun. Driven on at speed, clouds throw sudden shadow on the harbour water. Inattentive to what is after all a continual display, the citizens admire instead their fleets of sail. True, these too throw a dappled pattern and, better still, are tangible evidence of their own material virtue.

The mother found lodging on the north shore of the city's harbour and work on the southern shore, the city's centre. Impressive fast wooden ferries provided an excellent service between the two shores. They were double-ended with graceful sweeping lines, with full walk-round decks on two levels, and to avoid turning had wheelhouses at either end. A tall black funnel kept the smoke well clear. The speedy to-ing and fro-ing of these beauties was a pleasure to behold. Just yards from the shore the captain's telegraph rang down to the engine room for 'full astern' whereupon the ferry surged upwards several feet as the vessel's forward wake passed beneath. Foam boiled all about as the ferry ground into the buffer piles which groaned with anguish while above their heads the gangway slammed onto the wharf with complete indifference. Meanwhile workers pressed to be the first ashore. For many the prize was the certainty of a seat on the tram.

Once ashore, many workers would board another craft. This too was made largely of wood: a red tram. Lacking steam to blow whistles the trams could still stamp their authority with jangling bells, slamming, heaving, and lurching, just like the ferries. Unrivalled for transport and with priority on the road, they careered unmolested down the suburban hills, snapping and showering sparks just as they saw fit.

On an early boat home there was time to wander round and from the lower deck watch the stoker, stripped to the waist, making a good head of steam for the rush hour. Flame spurted as his shovel clanged on the hard bright coal. Facts forever intrude to compromise mystery, yet to learn that the boiler's steam drove a triple-expansion engine did not dispel the romance of the engine's beat. This was straight from Schumann's 4th Symphony.

The young woman, as one of this water-borne throng, found work as a hairdresser, an occupation in which she had been happily employed since her school days. She was obliged to work long hours, for part-time work was almost non-existent, much as were single mothers. To many, the young woman's circumstances were simply those of a single mother with the stigma that that then entailed. And her story was just that: 'her' story. As with her colleagues, she worked late on Friday night and Saturday mornings. Hard as it was, she needed the money.

The boy, at kindergarten, would recall blissful afternoon naps on mats under sighing pines close to a perfect beach. On the sand lay a full-scale mock pirate ship. To him it was very, very real. Outgrowing his pedal car – which had been ideal for ship-board driving on deck – he swapped it for a trike. Mother and son were lodged in an annex far from the main boarding house. Tucked in bed in the dark and tiny room, he must somehow accept that she must leave him to spend time with others. Frightened, and clinging to life's only certainty – his mother – it was time to learn that 'how-long-is-a-piece-of-string?' word, 'presently':

[Sob]: "When are you coming back?"

"Presently."

[Sob] "Yes, but *when*?"

"Presently."

The boy soon found that the perfidious subtleties of this word were of little use in this land of candid communication, and he never heard it again.

His mother worked in the salon of one of those department stores now sadly out of fashion, replaced as they are with myriads of small shops arranged in mazes that finally by way of punishment deposit the unknowing in unknown streets which intentionally lead one in an unhelpful direction. (No exaggeration is intended. No one is suggesting that the man who planned them did not know where he was going.) In contrast this most consumer-friendly of stores had a strongly collegial atmosphere among its friendly staff. Brightly lit on a winter's night, and with the best of merchandise, it made for a memorable sight.

The young woman noticed that people were friendly on first encounter, rather lacking in reserve and inclined to speak their minds. Her speech and accent grated on some and she felt it was intended that she should overhear remarks like "We don't have to live with the sound of that, do we?" Work in London's Mayfair had left its mark, although her own family made a more familiar London sound. Her father's tannery business was in the East End, to which he traveled from Hertfordshire each day. (After his daughter's precipitate departure the tannery was bombed flat, whereupon his son, with whom he worked, joined the army to help remedy matters.)

The boy eventually made visits by tram alone to see his mother at the store's salon. The gentlemanly lift-attendants who it seemed were chosen for their natural friendliness would direct him through the labyrinth. Once there, in shock, he would dive into and hide under towels piled high in a wicker basket. Girls, some of frightening beauty, made a fuss of him. Lively too; some liked practical jokes. Visitors might be offered 'Turkish delight' – old-fashioned solid green shampoo cut into squares and dusted with sugar.

Fate now intervened in the form of the Irish. The boy later came to see that only the Irish openness and sense of community could have wrought such sudden and unexpected changes in his life. Such events, he felt, could never have emanated from people other than the Irish. Their English counterparts were more withdrawn and less culturally and socially inclusive, because cohesion for the English was not a necessity.

It is onerous for people born in the only country they have known to be given the identity of a country quite unknown to them – that of their parents. These children struggle in their confusion. The English in their pragmatism brought their memories, discarding those unfavourable – for how could these serve them? They came for a better life and were occasionally conscious, too, that some might opine that they were there because they had not succeeded 'at home'. In contrast, the new generation of Irish very much retained their identity of origin. Common, however, to both racial groups as new immigrants, was that they on arrival had merely joined a club. Protests to the contrary by those most extrovert would largely go unheard by the already-settled throng.

The boy's mother worked with an Irish colleague. This gentle and devout woman saw that her friend was overstretched with the burden of a child and long working hours, so offered to help through her connections. Soon the boy was boarding with a second-generation Irish family. After some months, on turning five and becoming of school age, he attended briefly the local state school. Two older girls, a boy his own age, and their parents made up the household of three bedrooms. There was some estrangement between husband and wife, as the lady had a bedroom to herself. Between father and son there existed an almost cloying bond and they shared the second room. The new boy shared a bed in the third, placed between the two girls, who were seven and eight years older.

The breadwinner, who had served in the Great War and was now a manual worker, was well favoured with the new stuccoed semi-detached house. With half an acre of sunny, sloping garden it looked out upon an ever-shrinking dairy farm.

The boy of five could foresee its fate as the cows passed mournfully by the new houses. Thousands of these houses, proportionate and well-placed each to an almost-regulation quarter-acre, had been built just before the current war. They were the brainchild of a much-revered prime minister who, following the prevailing Keynesian economic and American New Deal wisdom, both provided much-needed housing and alleviated the huge unemployment of the Great Depression. The tenants paid rent to the state. Whether or not the inevitable currency inflation of the war ultimately paid for the houses is a matter for economists.

No doubt the boy's situation was seen as only temporary, as he was soon taken to a Catholic convent to board. His mother had expressed concern that the two girls might lay their limbs on him in their sleep. Possibly she had in mind the fact that at the age of two he had suffered from a hernia as a result of whooping cough. (As it happened the hernia recurred but the surgeon, his mind on golf or other things, stitched up the opposite groin. With time, as the lad lagged further and further behind his fellows, the problem was spotted at last and the correct side stitched five years later.)

This family was the focus of the boy's life when he returned to them for end-of-term holidays. With the Sisters of Mercy he soon experienced prolonged, almost constant religious ritual. Rising at six, the boys attended mass at once, seven days a week, with communion on Sundays followed by benediction. There were random musters at any time for the telling of the rosary. Nuns, as they walked about, would tell their rosary beads constantly. Boys to be viewed with a half-tolerant eye would be well advised to visit the chapel alone after class, 'visit' the 14 Stations of the Cross and pray before each one. Confessions were held weekly, with each boy visiting and kneeling in turn before the hidden priest in his booth. There then sometimes followed lengthy penances of prayer for the boys who knelt in the pews.

The neighbouring Franciscan friary sent a priest each day to take mass. Though the scent of burning incense swung through the chapel on chained censers may linger, it is as nothing to the remembered odour of the bacon and eggs awaiting the priest in the chapel's parlour. The boys then received their first meal of the day: a thin gruel of unhusked oats to be eaten – and all of it! – in strict silence. Ladling out this staff of life was a mental defective who was given shelter in return for considerable work. (Four decades later this exploitative practice was exposed in Southern Ireland.) With running nose the poor young woman would dribble the gruel over her thumb as she clutched at each bowl. The boy would be stood on a chair and caned on the backs of their legs if they as much as uttered a murmur. The scene faithfully followed Oliver Twist save that here no child, let alone Oliver, would want more – never mind risk asking for it. This 'breakfast' had to be eaten, as did what must pass for the two further meals of the day (Irish stew or tripe swimming in a gravy made with uncooked flour): perhaps the nuns were aware of some possible repercussions if the boys were to become hopelessly emaciated. Ironically, they came perilously close to this result through giving their charges a strong dose of senna pods every fortnight. Thereafter, the onward rush of 60 boys to the only lavatory, filthy and unlit, with just occasional scraps of soaked newspaper available – water and sewage everywhere – needs no further description.

As to the war, it was very much England's own. The nuns were from the Irish Republic and their nation remained neutral throughout. Furthermore, their government expected England's defeat. Inevitably there would have been some tension between the nuns with divided loyalties. The kin of some, perceiving the threat, enlisted with the Allies and so overrode their loyalty to the Republic. Their sister nuns in the majority were loyal to the rebellion, and had keen memories of the harsh repression of the British Black and Tans. It seemed to the boy (later, and admittedly in retrospect) that one or two of the former group had to endure the sentiments imposed by the latter. This they did in the generosity of their faith, aided by their wealthier and more cultured backgrounds. (To illustrate the situation further, it should be remembered that New Zealand's bishop had been tried for sedition for fomenting support for the rebellion. A dissenting jury allowed him to go free. The bishop held mass occasionally at the convent.)

America's entry into the war in December 1941, followed much later by attacks on Darwin and Sydney, sharpened realities if it did not modify sentiments. The boy recalled a few trips to the air-raid shelter because of some threat off the coast. Rationing of food and commodities was in force, yet it would be risible to imply that the boys' diet might have been better had this not been so. The nuns took their ration books with coupons for meat, butter, eggs, sugar, and clothing, and many a heavily iced cake was glimpsed through doors ajar as the nuns celebrated saints' days and their own birthdays.

Confined early to their beds each night, the boys were forbidden visits to the lavatory and were caned on their wet pyjama bottoms for ensuing accidents. A few boys were of wealthy parents who had simply placed them there the better to continue their own lives of luxury and ease. That there would be no school traceable with lower fees is at one with this attitude. To complement any such wish to be quit of their child, exeats beyond the gates were permitted on only one Sunday afternoon per month, with brief visits on the remaining Sundays allowed, when fruit alone could be brought to their incarcerated young. Boys attended the convent as day pupils too, yet for the inmates they were just disembodied elements from another world. They could not have imagined the lives of their boarding-school mates. Young children are insulated in part from misfortune and misery, in that they accept their situation, as they live it, is simply what life holds.

There are those of special talent to remember. A Chinese boy drew rapid non-stop action pictures of the war which unfolded like a newsreel. Having no toys heightened the capacity for make-believe. Aeroplanes and tanks were made from the core of a frond of Norfolk pine whose sticks stuck perfectly into acorns. The frond, too, would strip in one pull to make rapiers for Three Musketeers. Should a candle stub be procured from an altar boy, and somehow too a rubber band and cotton reel, then a moving tank would be contrived and climb any earthwork to destroy the enemy.

The convent with its small farm enjoyed a privileged site perched high on the isthmus above the harbours of the eastern ocean and the western sea. The huge western harbour lay beneath as if viewed from a dress circle. With none to tell him of its mysteries, the boy gazed for years in wonder at what was at last explained to him as the tide. Thus do explanations defeat magic for primitives. Trails of silvery light on water would stream to the land, pause and return from whence they came and just as they chose. On some days a toy ship would ride in too, seeming in some way to be part of this event. It would stay awhile and then without notice steal sadly away on its silver stream, leaving the boy with a sense of loss.

Along this prospect the convent's cows passed twice daily to milking. Without that dash of what these cows could offer, dribbled over the poor skivvy's thumb into porridge, the boys would have contracted rickets. Above this scene spinning swooping Tiger Moths and Harvards manoeuvred as their pilots trained for war, cutting their motors to stall and spiral down, the boys below awaited developments with interest.

Before the convent's entrance stood a grove of full-grown native trees which as evergreens throwing shade and too close to the building were considered a health hazard. The irony of this judgement could only indicate that these authorities had not seen the boys' living arrangements. The sawyers engaged to despatch the trees felled them and arrived at the last, a gigantic multi-limbed Monterey cypress or macrocarpa. It crashed and shook the ground as a dozen opossums were flung from their lairs and fled across the playing field.

The happiest moments in the boys' neglected lives were the occasional visits of a Christian brother whose arrival was announced by the tinkling of his Austin 7 as it struggled up the long drive. Ecstatic, the boys rushed from every direction shouting, "Father Terry! Father Terry!" Renowned as a storyteller, he would recount *Treasure Island* by heart in a pitch-dark annex. The rap of his stick for Long John Silver's wooden leg was frightening enough. When a startled opossum leapt from the wall and ran amongst the boys, chaos ensued.

The convent, an imposing building itself, was given an unwarranted and disconcerting dignity through its stately, park-like grounds. The dominant trees were huge oaks and Moreton Bay figs, these last with buttresses supporting ever-spreading limbs from which trailed curious aerial roots. In this setting cub and scout meetings were held by a Franciscan lay brother. Occasionally the boys cooked flapjacks of flour and water fried in dripping over a campfire. These almost-inch-thick items, topped with jam, were quite the best food the boys received and their starving stomachs accepted the ravages of the mixture without reproach.

Following meetings, boys were directed individually to visit the cubmaster in his friary cell. His own summons received, the boy, rigid with fear, was not a prospect and was quickly re-buttoned, but did receive the customary 'don't-tell' toffee. Every fortnight the boys were bathed by the nuns in baths set in rows, but here their subjects were ordered to cover their objects with flannels and there were no toffees. As to the friar, the more worldly day boys seemed unconcerned about his attentions and nicknamed him 'Carroty-man'.

There was relief at times from misery with the natural camaraderie of boys making the most of things in a shared situation. But for one particular subject the visits of his mother would rend him through and through. His sobbing and clinging at the convent gates disrupted what would have otherwise been a gradual conversion to the more cheerful state of an orphan. Pleading with her to take him away, without success, the boy came to see that relief from heartbreak would come only if she did not visit him at all. This of course she could not do, and so the situation continued.

Then one day it was enhanced with terror. His mother had happy memories as a day pupil at an English Catholic convent. So she felt quite at ease in telling the Mother Superior that she did not want her son converted to the Roman faith. As a result the boy, as the only non-Catholic in the convent, took part in all religious services except confession and communion. One fateful day when he was nine he was called to the convent office. Mother Superior's deputy angrily demanded that he confess to some unspecified offence. Accusations (never specified) continued almost daily for weeks – most frighteningly on chance encounters in narrow passageways. Other nuns, ever dutiful, seemed complicit in the matter, and passing her and the boy nodded sagely in support. Such was his terror and confusion he would have confessed to anything – but *what*? The accused in Kafka's *Trial* wrestling with unspecified accusations had the benefit of his maturity to help him seek reasons: but a child has only bewilderment which adds to his terror. At last, the devil must be thrashed out of him, so the big nun took the boy upstairs from where his screams might not be heard. Forcing him to kneel before her, she thrashed him with her heavy leather belt. This was to encourage him to 'confess', she said, and he could expect no peace until he did so.

The pressure continued until one day the boy chanced to notice the scoutmaster in the convent office. He had never seen him there before. The boy, whose constant crying and misery must have been indecorous, even in such a place, knew instinctively that the lay brother was there to suggest that he should be made to leave. Given the friar's proclivities, the now-unstable boy was a threat to him. The school year's end was due and the boy, still too unnerved to believe his good fortune, left. Guilt for unknown crimes and fears of threats and accusations have ever since haunted him. The legacy is one of defensiveness, lack of confidence, fear of failure and a dread of moving outward towards people.

The nuns, from poor rural backgrounds in the Irish Republic, were fervent soldiers for the faith. Their hierarchy received their unswerving obedience that displayed a tenacious acceptance of their vows. This was evident even to small boys. Above all, the nuns sought to impress on the children their view of the intense reality of sin. Never a notional concept, sin for them was as real as a brick wall. Beginning with original sin, Adam had eaten the forbidden fruit and man unless absolved through the faith must carry this curse to and then beyond the grave. Only baptism in the faith would remove this original sin, and only the practice of the faith would reserve for one a place in heaven thereafter. Venal sins – of the lesser kind that did not transgress the ten commandments – were more easily forgiven, but unconfessed and unrepented mortal sin sent the sinner if not to hell, at least to purgatory. Some nuns were lurid in their descriptions of hell. The shrieks of the damned as the flames licked around them convinced the boys utterly.

The nuns reserved their greatest hatred for the sin of pride. For them it was the concomitant of all sinful action. No doubt this assisted discipline in their hierarchy, as insubordination indicates pride. Family influences for most boys of course mitigated against the nuns' obsession. Although much admired for their devotion, family elders would intimate that the good sisters did not live in the real world. How boys were to gain self-confidence while forever worrying about pride remains a mystery.

Dominating everything was the sentiment of 'the weight of remembered oppression'. Sentiment defeats facts. Politics follow sentiment with only chosen facts in support. Irish and English history follow their entrenched positions of history on either side, as it has always been.

Simple nuns and small boys are long on sentiment and short on facts. Piecemeal knowledge of a subject that even perplexes academics was all they had. So, making the most of it, Henry the Eighth rivaled Lucifer and dominated sentiment to the extent that Oliver Cromwell's terrible record in Ireland was hardly mentioned. And now the nuns had relatives who had suffered through the Black and Tans. Yet once the peace treaty was signed and the British withdrew, the two Irish factions fell on each other. Members of the faction refusing the treaty terms were often executed. But the difference was that *that* was an all-Irish affair. It was always tragic that England's safety required that Ireland not be dominated by France or Spain.

Of Henry, the nuns said that upon his death he turned black. The boy was amazed, as he had recently seen his first dead body. A priest accompanied him to pay respects to the woman in whose family he spent his holidays. She lay on her deathbed, her face white, just like the sheets. Of course, the boy could not know she had been powdered white. Yet it seems the nuns may have been right: Henry rolled off the back of his hearse at Richmond, and as a hugely fat man his gaseous and bloated body exploded as it hit the ground, so he may well have turned black.

The boy was grateful for the nuns' strict view on theft: "Steal a pin, steal a bigger 'ting," they said in their Irish voices. Sadly, the nuns did not manage to explain that lies and deceit too were theft – theft of confidence between people. This awful truth did not strike the boy until decades later. Passing years saw the nuns' abhorrence of theft compromised by the world at large. Many educators in their political idealism described property as 'the fruit of theft', with the inevitable logic that property should be held in common. Short of applying this solution, such educators were deficient in basic economics, for to set a man to watch another is hardly a recipe for efficient production. Other refinements too became evident later with some who felt they could not understand the concept of theft until they had attempted and enjoyed it themselves: an act that cannot even be cloaked in the sentiment of 'stealing from the rich to give to the poor'.

Some boys went on to be successful in life and so shed the nuns' intense concern about pride. They discovered the assertiveness and self-esteem to support their endeavours. Worldly Catholic families admired the nuns' piety, content that it was unrealistic. They felt their support for the clergy gave them a bulwark against their own sins and some prospects for the life hereafter. Overtones of the sale of indulgences in pre-reformation times were still with us.

Not yet ten, the boy left the convent still terrified he would be pursued by Mother Superior wherever he went. In contrast, he was not anxious about the examination in the friar's cell; nor were the other boys, it seemed. In any case, subjugation in the convent was so complete that no child would be capable of formulating a complaint, let alone delivering it. Now, more than 50 years on, therapy specialists in 'retrieved memory' extract from 'victims' of sexual abuse details of offences from 30 years past which send offenders away for lengthy sentences. How oddly this sits with contemporary society where sexual perversion is advertised for sale in family newspapers. Any dispassionate observer may note that this license has its counterpart in furious reaction when the matter of 'consent' between parties is in dispute, even regardless of whether or not there has been a commercial transaction. All this is facilitated by the decline in settled cohabitation between the sexes, with consequent neglected children who might well be better off in a benign institution.

Fifty years on and some nuns go jogging or smoke and play cards. The Chinese boy and his friend would retain a different memory. As they scrabbled in the dust among the tree stumps with their acorn-and-stick make-believe toys, this was of nuns in ground-sweeping black habits with only the oval of their faces showing, framed tightly in stiff white buckram. For the boys there was sometimes just a glimpse of something else: lying prone in the dust they might catch a glimpse of a shaven head from under a stiffened cowl.

The boy spent holidays with the family, who sent him with their own son to visit farming relatives. The farmers were two 'boys', as Irish usage has it, who were both stereotypes of Irish bachelor farming brothers. The contented lives such men lived as sons of immigrants may have given rise to townsmen saying pioneers 'had the world by the tail with a downhill pull'. This envious observation reflected the fact that farmers enjoyed a guaranteed overseas market. Still, the work had to be done and its schedule well organised. On 100 acres of permanent pasture, the dairy farm mated its ten-month-milking-season cows to its Jersey bull. The heifer calves were sold or kept as replacements, while the males (bobbies) were taken each day during the calving season to the farm gate for collection and slaughter. The charm factor displaced this grimmer reality each morning as the resident horse drew the swishing sled of cream-churns to the gate. Cream only: there was no market for skimmed milk, which might be fed to pigs if there were any; if not, it was just run into the creek. The resulting whey formed thick slabs floating on the water. Huge eels as thick as a man's thigh chomped at this manna and paid no heed to children gaping in amazement.

As the farm's grass grew well for the ten months' milking no winter-feed root crops were grown and the herd was dried off as the grass growth slowed. No tractor was required, which in any case would destroy the pasture. So the horse drew the fertiliser box in early spring and slid the sled of loaded hay to the contented wintering cows. The bachelor brothers were as contented as their charges: they seemed not to have a worry in the world. Other than occasional visits from relatives they had no social life, but never missed a race meeting. One cloud appeared on the horizon before the boy moved on. The elder brother was aging, so to keep house they engaged a housekeeper – an Englishwoman who had served as an Army sergeant in the war. They were terrified of her.

Holidays were also spent with another branch of the extensive Irish family in a town nearby. One was blissfully long when all schools closed owing to a polio epidemic. It was felt that the lady of the house, a retired school teacher, would be strict and ensure that the boys did the correspondence lessons sent throughout the country. The husband of the childless couple took racing bets day and night from a hand-cranked telephone on a shared line. As this was illegal they lived in fear of the police. The wife sublimated her lack of fulfilment in life each week by rearranging the house furniture. Although within a township, the house still enjoyed the visits of the nightsoil men. In the dead of night the boy heard but never saw them. Several summer months without school would gladden the heart of any child. Endless tree-climbing, bike-riding, kite-flying, underground tunneling without restriction from this otherwise strict couple is a happy memory.

With two years of primary schooling to complete, the boy's new school was Church of England and the fees expensive. They could only have been paid through much personal sacrifice on his mother's part. The pupils were relaxed and self-confident. It seemed they had never heard of 'the sin of pride'. It was plain that their self-assurance was due to an awareness of their families' financial standing and social connections. The convent experience had left the boy with a bad stammer. He felt he was not at all safe from Mother Superior and things would be worse for him as he had escaped. Thankfully a kind master dealt with the boys who mimicked his stammer, and it passed.

Unlike the convent, where the boys, put to bed too early, were caned if they went to the lavatory and caned if they wet their beds, the new school was more relaxed. Indeed there was even some sexual precociousness as on agreed nights they behaved much as bobby calves or young lambs. The convent boy lay in his bed frozen with fear, amazed at these cavortings. The participants, with no sense of guilt, were devoid of embarrassment. In the adjoining bed lay a Jewish boy who was similarly horrified and bravely resisted all demands cruelly made by the rest. The greatest of his travails was being made to eat bacon and pork, contrary to his religion. But he had great inner strength and cried with rage rather than self-pity.

These events somehow passed and in a later dormitory gave place to more intellectual pursuits. One boy had a special talent and would invent and deliver seamlessly a serial story on motor-racing, made up as he went along. Every boy listened enraptured: it was utterly convincing. Outside in the corridor a young master would creep silently about. Was he intent on catching bobby calves or bent on visiting the pretty junior-house matron? Things were certainly different from the convent.

Towards war's end the boy's mother bought a cheap army-surplus hut and a lakeside plot on which to place it. Appreciating nature as she did, it was inevitable that she would attempt to escape from the city whenever possible. The plot was steep, and on delivery the driver had no option but to push the hut off his lorry whereupon it rolled down the hill and split in two. This was fortunate as the hut was of necessity altered and thereby made more attractive. All this, with financial hardship for the mother that can only be guessed at, was finally complemented by a beautifully made second-hand clinker-built dinghy.

With this new situation he grew away from the Irish family, and as there were no people nearby he now enjoyed or endured the existence of a solitary small boy. Inseparable from his dinghy, he would row the day long far down the lake, never tiring of the beauty of bush-fringed coves and white sandy beaches. Infrequently enough for it to remain a thrill, he might glimpse a flashing rainbow trout driving whitebait almost out of its own depth against the shore. The eight-foot dinghy was heavy and safe. Its extravagantly shaped frames allowed for billowy volumes known as 'a good turn in the bilge', which gave it special buoyancy. Too heavy to be blown willy-nilly, it was ideal for buffeting the short steep lake waves which lack troughs to allow most dinghies to rise and recover. Once or twice the boy, slowed by wind, failed to return before dark. Launches with lights swept the shores in search of him while he rowed up the lake's middle, homeward bound in the opposite direction.

Returned from the reverie of solitude, the child became petulant and capricious. For his mother, as a woman alone, he was her only company; she had to please and spoil him after his long absence. It was as if he was her favoured suitor. Undisciplined, he took full advantage, conscious that he was free of the nuns and the anxieties of living as a stranger in the families of others. In those days a woman alone with a child was socially isolated. Little more than a patronising comment was offered for her loneliness. Convention decreed that any honest questing male should be aware of her situation. She was married, and there was the spoilt child.

The boy could not see that his mother, even as a beautiful woman, lived a lonely life of complete neglect, enduring long years of abandonment. Even the nuns had each other's company. But on one occasion he glimpsed beyond his own world. They had made the long journey down to the bach by train and had hours yet to wait for the bus to carry them on. It was a sweltering Christmas day and essential to seek the shade of the town's park. They sat together with fish and chips in newspaper for their Christmas dinner. Aged eight, the boy chanced to see out of himself and sensed his mother's desolation. Only an intense distraction and stillness betrayed her misery, as he was never to see her weep. It was a moment when no child would reach his mother with a gesture of closeness. The boy soon returned to his centered self, as he held her responsible for his own misery. Taking stock, she sat quiet and still for an eternity which the boy always remembered.

Decades later he shared this moment with his mother, as the memory too had remained with her. Ever-romantic, she was to endure 19 years alone hoping she might yet be reunited with the man she loved, her husband. While a man may suffer loneliness, a woman suffers more as it is her nature to be valued, admired and better still, cherished, else she may feel keenly her neglect. Now, 40 years on, he heard his mother say, "Once women did as their husbands told them, but not any more." The 'no-turning-back' school had arrived long since, and neither consequences for single mothers' children at risk from sometimes violent drifting males nor general delinquency from children deprived of a father-figure could turn the clock back. For many women the change had occurred for every good reason.

Towards her boy the mother was impossibly tolerant, and he took every advantage. And as with the child, so with the world: she would set her broad jaw balanced with wide-set blue eyes and take it all on the chin. In the isolated cottage there were no neighbours or visitors: just each other for company. In the city his mother was known for her provoking sense of humour, so now with her boy there was much banter and laughter. Prematurely he was exposed to enough sophistication to make any child bumptious. They spent long evenings lit by a roaring paraffin pressure lamp. There was no electricity or wireless, just clouds of midges attracted to the light and the endless drone of mosquitoes. Water-rats discovered a strange structure in their territory and chewed steadily through its soft fibreboard ceiling – ideal for their nests. Sometimes their noses would appear through holes, which his mother would cover with sticking plaster. Splashes of blood dotted the walls and ceiling, as this was the age before insecticide. Retribution could only be had by swatted newspaper when the sated mosquitoes sat still, having had their fill.

Somehow, his mother had managed to take extended holidays to be with her son. An excellent cook, she kept the wood stove stoked and prepared rich meals which fattened the boy accustomed to a meager convent diet. He was soon covered in boils.

As to discipline, the over-tolerant mother was simply shouted down over any issue. What was she thinking of? Was it that her child was her own particular cross to bear? Unlikely: self-pity was not in her make-up. So the boy will never know, left cruelly with the image of his mother gazing into the middle distance. Incidents both sad and funny were not lacking. Without a teacher, the boy, though he fished the day long, could not catch a trout. In fact years passed and one would not come to hand. Worse, the girl across the bay, her father a good fisherman, would catch one just as it suited her. Humiliation and jealousy were his constant lot. He could only bite his lip, turn away and shed a silent tear. Rage was not appropriate: that would be saved for his mother when she got home. Did she in fact enjoy the drama? Once begun, fishermen's bad habits persist. It took years for the boy to understand that tight contact between rod tip and trout fly is essential, as any bow in the line absorbs the shock of the trout's strike and it shakes free.

Trailing a fly in the wake of his dinghy would counteract this problem (even unintentionally). Commendably sceptical of the tradition that 'no one fishes on his own doorstep', he decided to harl a fly in front of the cottage. Setting his mother in the stern to hold the rod, he sat himself to row from the bow of the tiny dinghy. Alone, he would have rowed from amidships but with Mother in the stern with the rod it was cramped, and were she to stand up they could fall overboard. The dinghy nicely trimmed, they set off. Everything went well except that with the cramped rowing position from the bow the oars could not be shipped quickly inboard.

Sure enough, the proverbial large solitary resident brown trout seized the fly and set off without a single pause in its run. Frantic shrieks to his mother to apply some brake to the reel went unheeded. Frozen with surprise, she simply held the rod aloft as the reel screamed. He knew if he rushed to the stern to grab the rod they would be tipped out. So the trout, unhindered, stripped the line from the reel down to the spindle where a poor knot failed and the line disappeared forever. The boy, still ensconced in the bow, was aghast while his mother, if mortified, gave no sign of it: she was as ever implacably calm. He screeched and railed at her for days.

Two happy years at the boarding school were at an end. His friends were all going on from the preparatory to its college. The junior school, where pride was not a sin but the anticipation of success, represented security and a good home. It was now lost to him. For reasons he could not fathom, he sobbed and dreaded leaving, yet well understood why he had cried for weeks to be freed from the convent. Summoned to say goodbye to the cold imported English headmaster, he received no good wishes and was made aware that his mother could not afford the fees for the senior school. She was too proud to write to her husband for the money, though he was well remunerated and this would have amounted to little more than the difference between the married income-tax rate he enjoyed, compared with the severe rate for a single man.

So his mother persuaded the family of his convent days to board the boy once more. From there he cycled each day to a state day-school. But time had moved on. The family's son with whom he had earlier been friendly told him plainly that he was not welcome. With their mother dead, his two teenage sisters endeavoured to keep house. The boy, as in earlier days attempted to make himself inconspicuous, remaining silent and creeping into corners like an anxious cat or dog.

It was still a time when adults did not welcome questions from children. Children were expected to live in their own world. The attitude of 'spare the rod and spoil the child' still prevailed. Aged eight in 1945, the boy was perplexed for months trying to understand what was meant by the Allies' endlessly repeated demand for an 'unconditional' surrender. The negative prefix foxed him completely: he thought that it meant surrender '*on* conditions' but months went by and the oft-repeated conditions were never stated. A request for clarification from an adult would have been thought precocious. Carefully keeping his own counsel, memorably, did not save him from embarrassment. For the father's birthday the boy bought a record of Elgar's 'Pomp and Circumstance' marches. It was a bad choice: the man took them in silence with a withering look. Having served in the trenches in the Great War, and as an Irishman, he had no sympathy for the sounds of Imperial grandeur.

Prior to the attentions of Mother Superior's deputy the boy had managed second place in a class of 40. The ensuing torment traumatised him sufficiently to secure a place only in the lowest forms of the private prep and then the state school.

He never achieved a place in the top stream. It is notable that there is seldom much movement between classes, and understandable that top classes get the best teachers. Some of his taught anything rather than their subject, and reminisced on life in general to a captive audience. Conformity decreed that a teacher's competence went unquestioned. The reaction of time brought the new virtue of tolerance as an ideal for 'liberal' living. Conforming hierarchies were made to yield. This in turn later resulted in social confusion and disorder, the reactive remedy being 'correct opinions'. So far, the persuasiveness of political correctness has not curbed high levels of crime.

At morning school assemblies one could see the boredom induced by conformity on the faces of masters lined up behind their headmaster who plainly they did not admire. It seemed he had been appointed for his academic ability (he had written a textbook) but was not a leader. In class, one master talked endlessly of his war experiences. One could sympathise: they had 'put the world to rights' and 'made it fit to live in'. In time, sudden unexpected change was the result of ever-increasing cynicism about the status quo the world over. Students rebelled, boycotted or rioted against outdated rigid curricula, overflowing lecture halls and inadequate staffing.

It became plain his presence was no longer acceptable among the family and he had to go. He lost all contact with them, though some happy memories remained. He was found a place at the school's own 'house' for boarders. These amounted to only one-eighth of the school's roll. The boys were from distant farms or the small communities that served them. There was the usual clannish solidarity among the boarders, who tended to despise day-boys. As with the main school, the leadership was uninspired. The old wooden buildings of the house were some distance from the school, which gave the boys some sense of independence. There was not the jail-like feeling of being locked behind gates. This meant that boys might encounter girls, although rules and tradition required that there should be no fraternising in the street. Each Sunday boys attended an Anglican church where rules were more relaxed. A boy, through his peers would be expected eventually (and if not, goaded), to accompany a girl to her home gate and then kissed decisively ('pashed' was the slang). Back at the house the boys awaited Romeo's return to hound him with approving chants of "Casanova! Caz! Caz!" The boy, his face flushed scarlet, would be quietly gratified that he was entitled to some self-esteem. There was no problem of boys at puberty showing an interest in each other.

Dances took place each year with similar girls' boarding schools. The boys sent flower sprays for their partners to wear and everything was formal and well conducted. Some hearty country girls could remove bottle tops with their teeth. Any romantic aftermath might result in inter-school correspondence, sometimes with ardent acronyms on the envelope such as 'LONDON' – 'Love O Now Darling Or Never'. Such bravado did not alter the reality that the back seat of the American automobile culture was still a few years distant.

Agreeable memories aside, there was the leaderless drift at the school that on reflection the boy would have been well advised to consider none of his concern. Without a relative to advise him, other than his poor mother who yielded to his will at all times, he made the foolish decision not to stay a further year at school before going to university. At one with the aimlessness in the school's direction was the lack of vocational guidance, which was for schools only just beginning. Boys did not approach masters for advice. They did not offer it and in any case a boy had to be spoken to first as masters initiated any discussion.

This is not to suggest that such discipline at the school was applied with success. The boy was shocked that a fellow boarder was suddenly expelled for persistent smoking, and just before national exams. To the young, addiction is purely an adult concept because it is only revealed for what it is by the passage of time. Considering that almost every master smoked, one pictures with confusion the spectacle of a man putting down his cigarette in order to give a pupil yet another caning for the same habit. This irony must have finally occurred to the authorities, as to keep themselves in countenance they threw the lad out. An added disgrace was that he was discreet, taking care to smoke only outside school bounds, hiding in culverts and suchlike while returning from the main school. Almost no other pupil ever saw him smoke, and he was caught only through the over-zealous efforts of prefects keen to present their quarry to their masters.

Our over-opinionated subject, together with his friend, reacted with horror to this incident that did not concern them, and the pair made the decision that if they passed their matriculation exams they would leave at the year's end. The next step was to visit the head housemaster. He was digging his garden, made no comment, and went on digging.

In the forties and fifties conformity provided society's cohesion and the new exciting materialism its dynamic. New and considerable material goods were evident and their attainment a prospect. The appetite for possessions now long-since thought essential was as yet un-jaded. The mere possibility of acquisition was exciting and motivating in itself. The parents of his contemporaries had in their own lifetimes only just embraced the chance of buying quarter-acre plots, building bungalows and living independently of their parents and in-laws, preferably in another suburb. Prized beyond compare was that mobile self-and-family display unit, the motor-car, but its availability was restricted by overseas currency restrictions which gave car ownership even greater status.

Despite the laudable if selfish desire for betterment, how pleasurable to recall some conventions of the times! Even men advanced in years rose to offer their seats graciously to the opposite sex and in the street doffed the ubiquitous grey trilby with a smile. Decorum also decreed that people should stop at the kerbside, remove hats and caps and pause until any funeral cortege had passed.

The overall hush that descended upon the land on the first day of each week is difficult to describe, as total quiet offers no display. Church attendance had scarcely begun its decline. Although slightly in the minority, adherents of the Catholic faith enjoyed more influence in society than their Protestant counterparts, as the latter did not speak with one voice. Sunday, generally, was still not yet seen as a day lost without cause to life's goal of material advancement. Good Friday in Catholic homes was spent in almost complete silence, and no meat was eaten on any Friday. To opine that the vast majority were law-abiding may invite an academic's wrath. Vexed by the folk memory of unlocked doors and rosier times, the academic blames the problem of selective memory. To which the response: revisionism is the academic's justification and stock in trade. However, one famous historian, Trevelyan, wrote that this period gave him much optimism for the future and remarked on the new-found civility between citizens in general. So for him, it seems, people's doors were indeed unlocked.

Enrolled too soon at university, the boy was confused and could not focus. He could not find the steadiness required to listen, take down, assimilate then at examinations return what had been proffered by the lecturer. Anxious and defensive, he became critical of the teaching when plainly just to re-present the notes when the time came was the essential path for all; his more mature friends told him as much. Somewhat cynically, long lists of set books accompanied the curriculum, but to consult them and submit material other than the lecturer's notes was not a good idea. Dissention and failure make good companions, and the boy was transfixed and demotivated by the fear of failure.

The boy had rowed at school and for a short time stroked the university eight until an unreadiness to follow the coach's instructions sent him to the bow seat. For the crew a week's training at his mother's lakeside bach 160 miles distant seemed an excellent idea and so with the boat installed on a lorry they set off. With a tent pitched for sleeping, the prospect was superb for rowing, the water being non-tidal and without current. Seven miles down the lake the petulant youth disagreed with his crew over something or other, swam ashore and eventually returned over farmland.

The crew were now but six, the seventh being obliged to ship his blade inboard to keep the boat's balance. Homeward they rowed, buffeted through the ribs by the oars' handles, through the sharp chop that arose. At last returned, the crew's captain – a qualified solicitor – seethed with rage and demanded that the offender be thrown out of both boat and club. It then dawned on them that the matter should be overlooked if their week's training was not to come to nothing.

He had little idea what to study. His fellows were quick to tell him he had little future in farming, lacking family connections and capital. As farmers' sons themselves they disdained the viable gateways into eventual farm ownership such as sharemilking, fencing and contracting in all its forms. So the boy, ever-impressed by those who professed to know, turned away from that option. In education these were golden years of opportunity. Benign paternalist governments of either political persuasion opened their coffers liberally for all forms of learning. Subsidised boarding in university colleges with tuition fees paid was available to all, without any means-testing for the parents of the better-off. The boy enrolled for law. He admired his sharply dressed career-focused colleagues who, to their credit, were lawyers even before they had passed their first exams.

This self–debilitating admiration in which he held his friends was not assisted by his sudden infatuation for a little pneumatic blonde. Law students worked in law offices by day with lectures in the evening, and the confident smiling girl approached him as he searched a title in the Land Registry Office. Anxious people are vulnerable to any approach from the opposite sex. Surrendering, they lose their self-protecting reserve and vanity and are then in a reactive defensive position. Smitten, he was soon swooning in endless reverie. Attending lectures together he could think of nothing other than taking the girl into the dark vacant lecture room next door. If only that professor would stop droning on! Deep rapturous kisses were adequate: his upbringing ensured that things would go no further. A year of this – his second in the same course – ensured that he knew less at the end of the second than at the end of the first. Examinations followed, his girl passed everything and the boy, now 18 and feeling distinctly ancient, was still in year one.

Ungallant, boorish behavior by the boy ensured the inevitable devastating departure of the girl, who went on to enjoy many adventures with a string of lecturers, to the admiration and envy of her friends.

The following year, although still grief-stricken, he managed to pass a couple of exams but, still affected by the event, made plans to leave for England. His disapproving mother did not learn of this until a week before he left. Luckily, her unhappiness was tempered by the sudden appearance of a widower. They soon married and spent many happy years together. It would be uncharitable to suggest that the gentleman had been emboldened by the departure of her disappointing son.

A student law clerk's wages were inadequate for saving towards a ship's passage so he spent his lecture times in jobs elsewhere. He found work on the waterfront, in wool-packing stores and a nail factory. This last was unnerving as he was the only male on the factory floor and surrounded by strapping, giggling Polynesian girls in floral prints and with hibiscus in their hair.

The times were memorable for prolonged industrial strife. The Waterside Workers Union insisted upon complete control of the nation's wharves by managing their supply of labour through a 'closed shop'. Manning numbers for each gang, working practices and the wage rate for any specific cargo were under the union's control. With labour thus restricted and the Port Authority occasionally refusing to yield to their demands, it is not surprising that ships waiting to discharge and load stretched in line beyond the horizon. The heaviest cargo, ironically requiring the least physical effort, was the most attractive to the men so they increased their manning levels under bogus criteria of tonnage handled and safety factors. Thus the pay was £2 per hour, equivalent to £40 today, for kicking two slings under a crated car for the crane to lift, while most of the handsomely paid gang were just spectators.

At the time, and with fine irony, £2 was the export value of one pound's weight of fine wool for the country's sheep farmers. Farmers had endured the depression of the 1930s and now expected to reach this market, so were exasperated by the constant strikes. Nonetheless, the 'wharfies' felt that right was on their side, if only because the boot was now on the other foot. This last referred to the shameful practice world-wide of men turning up on the wharves each day in the hope of work with many turned away (as they lacked an organised union) without a compensating retaining fee. For these men things had merely turned full circle and they were not giving an inch.

Among the public, only the farmers and the better-off were without sympathy for the wharfies. The sentiment of the rest was largely that 'every dog has his day'. Conformity and egalitarianism were the virtues of the times, while the poverty engendered by the mismanaged capitalism of the thirties was not a distant memory. At last the worst of the strikes went on and on until the union found a redoubtable foe in a prime minister who was a practicing farmer himself. His government refused to accept the ruling of an independent arbitration court without further undertakings from the workers who, incensed, took to the streets to be confronted by mounted police with the army in reserve.

As the union men took the well-paid work there was less for casuals who, as despised scavengers, were known as 'seagulls'. Prior to organising themselves into unions all wharf workers had been seagulls, with seldom enough work to go round. Now, with the strike, the seagulls were seen as strike-breakers, although the boy, a temporary seagull himself, had the usual left-wing enthusiasms of youth and was sympathetic to the union's cause. But he did not enjoy being bawled out by a drunken unionist on a trolley bus (which sadly had replaced the beautiful trams).

Union men the world over remembered their shared history from when they too had been seagulls. These events, now largely of folklore, were then a recent memory and had just been dramatised in film from Budd Schulberg's novel *On the Waterfront*. To get work men were forced to bribe criminal bosses who took a cut from their wages. Partly owing to this publicity, dock and wharf workers formed unions with an agreement with the stevedoring and port companies whereby any oversupply of labour caused by fluctuating availability of work would be compensated. Understandably, this was at a rate lower than that of those working. On the union side, abuse arose when they began to restrict the numbers of their union and, using their negotiated monopoly to provide the sole workforce, dictated pay rates and manning levels. The result was that, as they intended, there was no need for a non-working retained force, which vanished to become casual labour – seagulls – at the beck and call of circumstance. In a phrase 'the wheel had turned full circle'.

The legal department of the Ministry of Works was a backwater naturally removed from the influence of commercial considerations. It was a condition of employment that he should give six months' notice, which seems excessive. He simply boarded a ship during the office lunch interval, yet he would forever feel shame for slipping away without a word.

After two weeks at sea the ship paused off Pitcairn Island and the settlement's tender delivered telegrams, among which were two for the accused. One was from his mother and spoke reams with two words: 'Teddy boys', this being the appropriate term of disparagement at the time. The other was a request from the Ministry for a letter of resignation.

By chance, in the department, the boy had had the good fortune to occupy the desk next to that of a distinguished gentleman. Although not aloof he rarely spoke and was burdened with work which he readily undertook as he could not genuinely share in the interests and banter of his colleagues. Such was the dignified though kindly bearing of this man of over 60 years, that all refrained from inquiring about his life in his native war-ravaged Poland. Finally, and discreetly, one learnt that he had been the Polish equivalent of a Prussian junker and governor of a rural province. Following the annexation of eastern Poland by the Russians and western Poland by the Germans under their secret pact, two thousand Polish officer prisoners mysteriously disappeared. For almost 50 years the Russians succeeded in blaming the Germans for the atrocity whereby the officers had been shot and buried in the Katyn forest. As with most Poles, this man knew differently and on the reconstitution of post-war Poland and having survived a Siberian prison camp he was delegated to interview Lavrenti Beria, the notorious Soviet Interior Minister, who denied all knowledge. Preferring not to live in a communist Poland, he led a group of compatriots overland to a new country. In a time of greater social discretion his hosts refrained from asking why.

Thrusting lawyers as opposed to circumspect career solicitors are not generally found in government legal offices. For the former, legal and commercial life go hand-in-hand. "A real lawyer," said a Danish colleague to the impressionable boy, "must be in love with the idea of transaction." Embarked on a law degree late in life, his friend had difficulty in sustaining interest in study, although he was conscientious in office work. Danes are renowned for celebrating the absurd. Incongruities normal in our use of idiom, embellished with picturesque antipodean metaphor, sent him into paroxysms of laughter. Commonplace advertisements advising that 'only live wires need apply' and similar were too much for him. Stocky and round-faced, he would heave with mirth and cover himself with cigarette ash. The boy was hugely entertained and was convinced that his friend was the first man ever to observe that 'You can't buy money with happiness.'

His colleague was divorced from time and place, and given his history it was not surprising. Aged 16, he had been on board the training ship *Danmark* when his country was suddenly occupied by the Germans while the ship was under full sail for the US. Most of the young cadets were taken in by wealthy American families but this comfortable fate held little interest for him so he went straight back to sea as a deckhand. With the huge numbers of ships sunk, it soon became time to abandon his own. One of his recollections was of a cargo of railway lines blown skywards, only to fall back, pierce the decks and twang like tuning forks. The attacking planes returned to strafe the ship and then released streams of toilet paper. He only told such stories at the boy's urgent prompting: cultured people seldom respond to questions on a subject as horrible as war.

The two strolled together along the wharves among the ships and fishing boats in their lunch hours. His friend's wide experience of life could not fail to make the youth aware of the limited horizons of his own existence. Though careful not to press any undue influence, his considerably older friend encouraged him to question whether law studies were his best option in life. The sophistication and style that leapt from the pages of *Harper's* and *Vogue* captivated him. Could he not be part of the act that displayed these beautiful women and the creations they wore for the world?

A boy may not go away a donkey and come back a horse, as the eighteenth-century country parson said. But nature did not decree that youth should take heed, nor imagine this reverend might hope to greet a troop of beaten donkeys! Further, worldly-wise cynicism ill becomes youth, being hardly a stage beyond disgruntled adolescence. Youth has not yet had time to observe that people and places are much the same the world over. In time, and with an eventual return, the sameness too is in the change. On returning, buildings that were once proud emblems of confidence now sit and cringe as relics preserved at the feet of towering blocks. Iconic buildings, monuments to the past humbled and in deep shadow, glance at the sheepish wanderer returned. Together they share the same chill.

Landmarks and buildings, though inanimate, were the signposts of certainty: they had endured for generations. Equally, the human point of reference was the family. What did the family think? Who did the family know? What would they say? What would they do? What would they advise? Individuals, almost universally, might make an independent decision to which the family was averse because of or despite the family's views; but they would not flounder in a void with no point of reference but their own. As with the landmarks, so with the family. It is no longer electorally viable for prospective governments to endorse the western nuclear family as the sole (and thereby preferable) situation in which to bring up children. Are the alternative structures viable?

So the youth prepared for his venture without the counsel of any circle or acquaintance other than his friend. Disapprobation there may have been with regard to his behaviour towards his mother, but nothing was said. For the time, his (and their) situation in life was unusual. Latterly, he lived just here and there but would turn up and with her tacit consent dip into her hairdressing takings. It was the grim melody that plays when any single mother's son holds her to ransom for his affection, and evidence again of the unequal struggle a single mother has to help her boy turn into a man. Disrespectful as he was to an extent that shocked others, his mother enjoyed the banter. It was the price she paid for the laughter they shared.

One telephone call was received in an attempt to dissuade him from leaving. No doubt the gentleman had been prompted by the boy's mother. As the husband of his mother's old friend, he had been pressed into service although the boy scarcely knew him. Ironically, the boy had visited her friend earlier; she had phoned and asked him to call. The lady, his mother's colleague from times gone by, was now financially comfortable and his mother seldom saw her. She felt it her duty to draw his attention to his mother's heavy workload. It was true: in addition to taking hairdressing customers at her flat she had been working late at nights coaxing sisal into fashion wigs for the heads of plaster mannequins seen in shop windows. Nylon wigs were not yet available and sisal was almost impossible to wave.

He arrived as arranged to find the lady clad only in a light morning gown. The beautiful woman moved gently towards him. With barely time to make his apologies the youth took fright and fled. He did not mention the incident to his mother except to say that her friend felt she was overworked. With the prescience of mothers she warned him that her friend's husband would not approve of his visit. The boy thought her comment so strange and out of character: he had never received the least advice from her.

The loss of his girl debilitated the youth. Months of grief turned well beyond a year – a measure which to the young can mean a lifetime. No elder male figure was available to encourage and shame him into 'getting over it'. Absurdly, there was only guilt, despair and humiliation. Yet such subjects are condemned to stumble on something new: a girl who will have not the slightest interest or sympathy in his parlous condition and then distracts him from the enjoyment of his self-pity. Enter a tall, perfect clothes-horse: a brunette with style and sophistication. Such was her poise that a callow youth in her company could pretend to some urbanity. Calm and discreet in her opinions, she was the perfect foil for a strident youth. So tractable and even was this girl's temperament that her perfection could, without quibble, only point to finality. Finality frightens the young (and even ancients resent its implications) and cruelly only added to the youth's resolve to board the ship. He would sail away and learn to design and make clothes for ladies like her.

Sadness at the parting did not deter her from stealing aboard early to place a beautifully dressed girl bear on his bunk. Five other cabin mates too must have sensed the romance of the gesture, for he was not mocked for it. His mother, rightly disapproving, did not attend the ship's departure. He heard that she waved a tea-towel from the hill on which she lived as the only link to her past callously slipped away.

The son was soon relieved to learn that his mother had found happiness with a cheerful, outgoing widower. He was childless and though they both now remained so, their greatest joy was to welcome the children of the neighbourhood. They especially offered friendship as such couples sometimes do to any that were taking temporary refuge from their own parents. Their children's Christmas parties held each year became a legend.

His mother's love of children remained to the end in a small family-run rest home where every kindness was forthcoming. It adjoined a school playground where, within a few feet of his mother's window, sat a trampoline. The school holidays did not deter two little girls from coming to play. Unknowingly, yet in a fitting salute she would have applauded, they leapt, bounced and shrieked together at the very instant she died.

The *Rangitoto* carried farmers and their wives home on the sheep's back. With the finest wool at £2 per pound owing in part to the Korean war, and competing synthetics still in their infancy, their ship had come home. This rush of sudden wealth enhanced their sense of worth and a capacity (at least in their wives) for censure. Yet to be fair they had been tested by years of waterfront strikes causing disruption to their exports. With a degree of rectitude scarcely imaginable even then, or indeed earlier, the ladies insisted that all decks be deserted by ten o'clock. Many passengers on this voyage of four weeks were in their late twenties and thirties. They could not even lean against a rail and gaze upon the waters. The ship's officers, with their own cabins, were not so incommoded, and the smirks they directed at their male colonial cousins testified as much. Rebellion against such coercion was still ten years away and the reign of the colonial matriarch was well entrenched. Their stature arose because in the new pioneering countries where men outnumbered women their involvement, especially in farming, was invaluable. No doubt some of these matriarchs of the fifties became feminists in the seventies, choosing thereby a different mode to exert their authority. (The pre-eminent exponent among modern feminists sought an audience and residence in the old country where they hadn't heard it all before and where she stubbornly remains.)

Competition with the airlines had scarcely begun. Such a long flight was expensive although workers soon made the calculation that four weeks' travelling with loss of wages added to their bar bill would have more than bought an aeroplane ticket. No attempt was made to visit ports en route for the diversion of the passengers, although this soon changed when the shipping lines found that aeroplanes were serious competitors. Apart from a brief compulsory disembarkation at the Panama Canal and a refueling stop in the Dutch West Indies, where passengers were discouraged to land, nothing was offered. So the ship puttered across two strangely calm oceans while frustrated males spent their money on a strange new warm flat and sticky beer. Our ever-hopeful was heartened for his future plans by winning the fancy dress competition. Luckily the crew did not compete: that homosexual stewards held fully-dressed weddings below decks had been known for years. It is doubtful that he could have rivalled their talent and experience. How strange that such matters were beyond the knowledge and censure of the sheep farmers' wives who patrolled the decks above.

Seventeen years on from 1940 the Panamanians were happy once more to accept sterling. So poor were these citizens that ancient buses stopped unbidden in the hope that a solitary pedestrian might climb aboard. The youth wandered into a darkened bar. Reflection from bottles and glasses seemed the only source of light. A welcome chill and total quiet gave the bar its style. With sudden and dramatic effect a deep, resonant voice supplied the perfect foil. A negress dressed in black sang, yet could scarcely be seen. Only the glint of flashing teeth and sheen on her lips and tongue gave her away. With arrogant and husky nonchalance she sang 'That old black magic'. The song and its delivery were for the mature and confident; its sensuousness beyond his experience, even comprehension. It gave him a sense of dread.

His idea on arrival was to contact his mother's father, then find work of some kind and through evening classes eventually arrive at his goal: making beautiful clothes for beautiful women. Of course his mother had no part in these plans beyond supplying her father's address. The vagueness of the young man's intentions disturbed a fellow passenger, a charming old gentleman who took endless pains and every opportunity to insist that the youth contact his father. At opportune moments the gent returned to the subject, but the youth was most reluctant to comply and pointed out that he had received only one letter from his father in his life, and that furthermore his embarrassment at making an approach would be acute. But the gent would have none of it and the youth, flattered by the attention, yielded and sent a wireless telegram two days out from Southampton. Shortly, a reply was received: "Welcome, you will be met at Waterloo Station."

Once ashore, our subject's first meeting was with a smartly dressed young Customs officer who asked, "Is that all you're bringing to England: a suitcase full of dirty washing?" Laundry facilities for six-berth cabins were not prominent, although it had been indicated that a laundry was down some corridor somewhere. It seemed logical to accumulate things and launder them on his arrival. But socially, conversationally, here was something new. No matey, laughing banter that oiled the wheels of social exchange as it did from whence he came. It would take time for him to understand that here there was a new dimension, a certain coldness masquerading as reserve which at worst could seem officious. Fifty years on, the subtleties of the class system remain, though diluted by considerations of merit and wealth. At that time, an Australasian would be outgoing indeed, a parody of himself to the point of brashness (never mind bravery), to ignore the implications of the British (pointedly, not just English) class system. How to adjust, spotting signposts, assessing implications of distance and reserve, could be a slow process. A casual humorous remark, thought flippant, at worst bumptious.

The journey to London on what was known as 'the boat train' shocked him. Generally, he had thought a 'green and pleasant land' would unfold. Often the train passed between opposing back yards. Grimy brick houses as if in shame turned their backs one to another but to little purpose: they were joined to their neighbours in endless lines. He learnt that such 'terraces' existed in Australia, but that too was a country far from his own. And then, how could such a reserved people be responsible for this shrieking gutter press? The only newspaper he had known was so lofty that even the word 'pub' was placed between inverted commas.

At Waterloo, his friends of four weeks took their leave, the platform slowly emptied and he found himself alone. Suddenly a uniformed person appeared, who quickly seized his suitcase and dumped it on a trolley. The case's fastenings yielded to this exertion and the offending linen appeared once more. He was unaware that this man was called a porter but it was obvious that he expected some sort of instruction. They waited together in silence for the proverbial eternity. There had to be a limit to the number of times he scanned the deserted platform in exaggerated fashion. To heighten his embarrassment the train shunted away – taking, he realised, his regulation trilby with it. Bare-headed now, he felt doubly exposed. There was still no-one in sight and this man with his case would expect to be paid. But to do what? To go where? A poor money manager, he nervously fingered his remaining half-crown. He had however sent a small letter of credit in advance to a London bank but now realised it was Friday evening so there would be no money till Monday. His mother's father lived many miles distant ... there seemed nothing for it but to move slowly towards the platform entrance murmuring something or other to this man who still had his case.

The platform appeared to have a gate. He had only known platforms completely open to the station. To him, the message 'You will be met' meant surely to be met at the train itself. He had no alternative but to pass through the gateway, where a small respectable lady approached and inquired, so formally, if he were Mr. Waddington? This felt-and-feather-behatted person stood a good chance that he was as there was no one else around. She was, she said, to take him somewhere by cab. He felt bound to tell her that he had no money but she assured him this was not a concern. Much relieved, he handed the porter his half-crown.

He assumed the lady was either a friend or employee of his father's, although he was bemused (even by the standards of lessons yet to come) by her formality. She explained that she belonged to a firm called Universal Aunts, but sensibly did not elaborate upon the firm's concept or function to such unpromising material. The destination, a gentleman's club, loomed at last and the 'aunt' departed, having bade him enter to await his father.

The club had the first revolving door he had ever encountered. In theory it should be impossible to come to grief on exiting it, but he stepped out too late and, attempting in some panic to reverse its turn, he fell over his suitcase. There was no injury, only embarrassment as he was deposited at the feet of yet another uniformed person. Within eight hours he had encountered five uniforms: ships, customs, railways, porters and now that of a sergeant in the British Corps of Commissioners. The sergeant surveyed the scene. Perhaps he had not seen such a display since the war service in consequence of which he had been given his present position. However, the offending suitcase was stowed and the visitor directed to wait in the library.

This vast sombre cavern had a ceiling as high as a cathedral and a religious hush long since gone from libraries. In deep armchairs, their working lives over, sparse club members slumbered. Displayed throughout were the memorabilia of the 'father' of the 'mother of all parliaments', William Gladstone. Statues of the great man gently declaimed that finally only his own convictions were tenable.

With neither expectation nor trepidation (much as a youth's optimism is its own reward), the youth waited for what he imagined would be a casual if novel rather than a salutary meeting. After some minutes his father appeared. There was no problem in identifying him, as his mother possessed a serious profile portrait of the style common in the thirties. The photographer had seen that his subject showed to advantage in profile. He was dark with an Errol Flynn moustache. His first remark was what anyone would expect for the occasion and delivered in a friendly manner: "When I last saw you, you were this high!" Following which the next statement was most unexpected: "If you've come here to disrupt my forthcoming marriage you can turn right round and go back to where you've come from."

Although this was only one more in a day full of surprises, this utterance would have had less impact had it been delivered as an outburst. Instead the tone was cold and even. Dumbfounded, with no knowledge whatever of his father's personal life, he could only murmur, "Of course not." Perhaps even at that time an affronted, even angry response on his part would have been appropriate, but he was too much taken aback. His failure to react handed his father the initiative. Someone of a different stripe might have taken umbrage and stalked off. Yet this was a time when the young deferred to their elders and the subtle consequences were that he was now less his own man, and no longer free and accountable to himself.

His father asked what his plans were. On explaining that he intended to stay with his mother's father, find a job by day and go to night school, the reply came, "That won't be necessary." Startled and speechless, the youth thereby forfeited his independence and whatever cheerful self-confidence he possessed.

The fear that was part of him had at least never kept him from independent action. The person before him was of a kind he had not encountered before. In a long day of many uniforms, had this man worn one signifying the utmost authority, the interviewee could not have felt more subordinate. Cold English reserve, if ever encountered within his own country, was thought at best just a humorous anachronism or at worst a dishonest display of imagined social superiority. The affable, confident American as diffused by Hollywood was the role model rather than his English counterpart.

The exchange stunned the youth. In seconds he had been stripped of his faculties. Though generally perceptive, he had failed to see that despite the welcoming telegram he was in fact unwelcome. Naivety had led him to take the message at face value. Moreover, no mature mentor was on hand to explain that his unexpected arrival from the distant past could understandably be unwelcome. Only after some years and with hindsight did the son detect in this tense, unsmiling man the inherited signs of congenital anxiety. Fear of failure alone drove him to success. As the man chain-smoked, drawing deep into his lungs all the drug could offer, the youth should have perceived that a friendly relationship was unlikely. Anxiety and hesitancy were now his own lot, with all personal initiative surrendered for what was made plain; his own good. Shortly thereafter his father told him to address him as 'Sir' – an epithet even then already outdated by a generation.

Soon they were driving through London, then beyond and south. It occurred to him that his intention had been to go north, to his mother's family. But it did not strike him that his intentions and decisions were now a thing of the past. The silence was palpable and the icy atmosphere such that his attempts at conversation drew no response. As this tactic of polite intimidation and punishment was successful the young man took refuge in the memory and habit of his childhood, whereby as an unwelcome boarder in other people's houses he had pretended himself invisible. This strategy had never worked before and he could see it wasn't working now but it was the best he could do.

Passing into that fringe of country that genteelly flirts forever with the town, they eventually drew up to some imposing buildings the like of which of course he had never seen before. He learnt that these were the gate, lodge and coach house to what had once been a grand estate. His father rented the top flat in the coach house, known as 'The Hayloft', as in horse-and-carriage days this was what it had been. On entering, the general tension, if anything, increased. An attractive girl in her early twenties was present, and though she offered a friendly greeting she was self-effacing and subdued. It was not evident at the time but became apparent later that this young woman, who was less than half her protector's age, was his intended bride. However, a problem remained in that her suitor had been married in 1935 and remained so, to his son's mother, at that moment in December 1957.

Divorce remained unusual and frowned upon generally by those who were not of the stage or screen. The grounds for obtaining it were very restricted, and there even existed an official known as the Queen's Proctor who in some instances could oppose petitions for divorce. At the time the youth's father had recently ended a long relationship with a cousin – a doctor – in favour of this girl at that moment in his company. To illustrate the contrast with the standards of today, owing to his connection with the girl a photograph of the father had graced the entire front page of the nation's main tabloid. The youth learnt much later that the girl, who was then aged 19, had fled a disastrous marriage with a Guards officer. The reasons for her so doing could not in those days be made public, with the result that the father was successfully sued by the husband for 'enticement' and made to pay substantial damages; hence the publicity.

The girl was not long out of school, and having abruptly left her husband she lacked any means of support and (ironically unbeknown to the youth at the time) on advice approached the genteel Universal Aunts for help. Thus she became secretary to his father (who later in life admitted graciously that he had a reputation for 'taking secretaries under his wing'). The attractive, intelligent girl quickly became indispensable to his business of distributing industrial detergents and inventing and manufacturing systems to dispense them. She had poise, quiet confidence and a gift for figures. At a time when there were still few women in business, men responded with chivalry, doors opened on every hand and the enterprise flourished. It only remained for such a formidable union in business to be reinforced by marriage. And for this vibrant couple, further good fortune followed. Not long after the youth's arrival, his mother, after 19 years of desertion, petitioned for divorce, having herself accepted a proposal to marry. As a result there was no requirement for her husband of 22 years' duration to pay her any alimony, and he soon remarried in turn.

Despite an intense devotion to each other and the nervous tension between them giving thrust to the business, the new relationship became difficult. In terms of marriage as her husband understood it (and indeed as it was still widely understood) he insisted that his young, highly intelligent wife should defer to him in all things. Any expression of anger on her own part was totally foreign to the girl: she had no need for it as a tool and plainly saw its display by others as pointless. Her husband's motivating forces – anxiety and fear – now had greater scope: she was now both his secretary and wife. But fear is often the expression of insecurity, exhibited by visible lack of confidence. Explosions of anger are expressions of the problem and are often unconvincing. And so the man drained the suppressed resources of the young woman, who left him to join the ever-lengthening queue of petitioners for divorce.

But all that lay in the future. For now, at the end of this unnerving and astonishing day, the young man stood at a back window of the coach house overlooking a rose garden. His father was absent (in accord with the decorum of the day the suitor had accompanied the young lady to her home) so he was able to relax. In the fading dusk that just precedes twilight he was presented with new sights as a comfort from the experience of the day. Light reflected from cloud over the great city to the north, mingled with remnants of sunset, and this light in turn was caught by snowflakes pointedly but gently falling on their own terms. They fell to make that special blanket of quiet that snow alone provides, and to enhance the few remaining roses – always the most romantic, and unlike those that shout in summer. Even the garden's slight neglect was of comfort, as if to quieten the fears of those who might only manage to saunter through life.

Unfolding time demands optimism from all for the next unknown moment. It is mostly personal vanity that in retrospect recalls embarrassment. Confined in the little flat which despite its desirable locality could never disown its origin as the place where the coachman kept his hay, the trio ground out the interminable and distractionless Christmas and New Year. How helpful it would have been if some divine counselor had advised the couple that the girl could never sufficiently surrender her psyche to calm the man's fears – she must forever give more. The three walked on eggshells, although the older man took it as his prerogative to break a few. But generally it was quiet and the ticking clock was dominant. In the evenings a man and his dog entered the television and spoke the news. Things were not quite as they seemed: the dog with smiling candor looked straight at the viewer while his master, the reader, read his script from somewhere above the viewers' horizon. The audience was appreciative, however, as the man went on to run the entire BBC. This brief diversion aside, the youth may have suffered less than his companions in confinement. Once again he found himself in other people's houses: his situation was at least familiar.

With all personal initiative abrogated on his own part, the youth was (circumstances pressing) found a room at the old YMCA in the West End. Much persuasiveness plainly was brought to bear, as accommodation was short everywhere and the hostel had a long waiting list. His room-mate, an Irishman, somewhat older, was of a type he had not encountered before. Ascetic in features and appearance, he was not so in general demeanour. Tall, slender and languorous, he had the whitest of skin and the blackest of fine hair. As a librarian with some breadth of knowledge, he could hardly avoid humouring the newcomer. Through many layers of subtlety he contrived to conceal the fact that he disliked the English, but just on occasion he could not resist making it apparent. The onus was on the new room-mate to discover this and to reflect how sad it was that this person should choose to live in a country whose people he disliked.

The art school, where a training in fashion could be followed, was just down the road. Having some qualifications from university, the young man was accepted for entrance on the strength of a drawing. This was encouraging: he had never drawn anything before. Pattern-cutting, dress-design and fashion-drawing from a model filled the day with eventual goals a perceived prospect. But complexes born of a three-year age difference, the strangeness of the country and the other-worldliness of his fellow students perplexed him. Despite pursuing the course adequately, fear of failure once more offered its throttling grip. Fright and anxiety drove him to consider returning to what was supposedly home. Behoven to a virtual stranger, his father, for his living allowance, he felt keenly the burden of obligation. To reappear shamefacedly from whence he came (these being times when the 'overseas experience' was unusual) was almost as unattractive an option as remaining. In any case he had no money for the fare. Failing to make friends among his fellow students, he had nothing at day's end other than the prospect of seeing his chalk-white and thin room-mate stretched out on his bed looking as if he had spent his whole life under a sodden log.

For all that, he was keen to learn about fashion, who is a demanding and changeable mistress. Her authority flows sometimes from indeterminate sources yet must be obeyed. As a relief from her dictates, the students held a weekly dance in almost total darkness with both sexes clad in pyjamas. The youth got no further than the door and recoiled in horror: he felt as old as Methuselah. Socially, it did not help that the college lacked a canteen. A two-course hot meal could be had for two shillings in a back street. He was startled to see the occasional gentleman dining in an overcoat and wearing a bowler hat. Conversely, such persons were affronted by antipodeans eating pies at food stalls: "Ain't y'ever 'eard of a knife and fork?" Certainly such gents were dressed for the weather, whereas the outsider thought he could continue wearing the jumper knitted by his girlfriend of the teddy bear. That winter saw the last of the infamous Great London Smogs before the clean air acts forbidding open fires brought about an improvement. He was racked with the desperate cough that afflicts careless students. Other sights startled him: beggars, prostitutes and determined gypsy women pressing heather on the unsuspecting.

The son's arrival provided impetus for his father to reconnect with his own family. His sister said she had not seen him for 20 years. But as part of the eternal mystery of families, as viewed by the non-familied, it did not seem to matter. Be they seemingly indifferent towards one another to the unfamilied outsider, their identity whether they disclose it or not is mysteriously under their own control. The sister thus became an aunt, the first the youth had met. This kind though formidable lady had been widowed early in married life and leased a large rectory near Oxford. She boarded students who attended the university, as did her own son. Perhaps not inappropriately (all things considered), the aunt vouchsafed that her unexpected nephew "might have been a lot worse". She had two very bright children. Her son, a year younger than the visitor, had almost finished his degree. His sister, a little older, had finished hers and had become secretary to the country's pre-eminent atom scientist. Occasionally, brother and sister would leave messages in Greek to each other on the kitchen blackboard. The visitor had no difficulty in feeling inadequate.

Understandably, his kindly host and kin provided in themselves a greater field for his own observation than he provided in himself. They lived in their world and any individual outsider could only be an object of occasional speculation as to his background and sentiments. As observation is often flattered by hindsight, the truth of accumulated impressions is compromised. One is then left with a consensus of generalities finally accepted by most. Thus hindsight offers explanations for men's memory of events.

It seemed the country's large population jostled rather than bustled about their business. They were subdued and their surroundings bleak. Meat had only just ceased to be rationed. As to the adornment of the female body, Dior's 'New Look' gave elegance to the ultra-slim and wealthy, but the long, voluminous sweeping skirts with little pinched jackets could never do much for the masses. The prevailing mood was an indication of how the people viewed themselves and their situation. Sullenly, they considered they had 'won the war and lost the peace'. Conditions for post-war German workers were already superior to their own and Europe was benefiting from the generosity of the American Marshall Plan. Although grateful to the Americans, the English considered the US had come late to the Second World War, as they had to the first. The United States had then insisted that the 'lend-lease' repayments for war material prior to their entry into the conflict should be honoured. Britain then bled to support the pound at an unsustainable level for over two post-war decades to meet this commitment.

Other than the drain on resources endured through two world wars within 40 years, two further influences sapped the morale of the people. First, rapid withdrawal from the burden of Empire could hardly enhance the nation's self-esteem, and the second factor was the 'we-are-the-masters-now' effect. The socialist programmes of free national health, unemployment benefit, pensions, subsidy and nationalisation of unprofitable industries relieved workers' anxieties at a certain level, but were too expensive and the nation could not prosper. Taxation to assist in funding rose to a super-tax level of more than a pound due on a pound earned. Landed gentry were stripped of their properties through death duties if they could not muster sufficient funds to pay these for the property to pass to their children. Exchange controls were imposed to prevent the flight of capital whose owners sought to escape this punishing regime. Naturally, all this pleased most those who had elected these new masters. The new arrival overheard one poor and old man say to another, "Well, the wheel has turned full circle now!"

It was fortunate for the country that at the time the price of imported commodities, especially food, was low. Had this not been so, social unrest with strikes to meet food-price increases would have forced an international sell-off of the pound, forcing a devaluation at home and a failure to meet US debt repayments. Concerning devaluation, the country much later learned the lesson that the value of any country's currency must truly reflect the international sale value of its goods and services. Two post-war decades plus two hefty devaluations passed before the pound was allowed to float so the world could decide what it was worth. Nevertheless, before this came to pass, inflation was kept at bay by extreme fiscal and monetary austerity, despite the profligacy of near-Utopian social programmes. As late as 1963 German economists visited Britain to research the admired stable currency. The price paid for this achievement, however, was too high, and against the hardest of currencies the pound's true exterior value tells its own story: 19 Swiss francs to the pound in 1951, nine in 1969 and three in 1979.

At a distance it seems remarkable that a considerable part of the resigned disgruntlement in the population could emanate from a misconception. Under the well-worn principle that it is best to tell the people what they want to hear, politicians and the press continued to affirm that Britain, the dominions and Empire plus the Americans, with some help from the Soviets, had won the war in Europe. More than two decades passed before the population were disabused of this view, and that the preponderance of effort to defeat Germany lay rather with the USSR. The country's leaders and newspapers had some small excuse in that the intensity of the Cold War was such that historians could not gain access to comprehensive information. Generally, too, it was not an easy task for the news media to explain that the Russians, who were by then the enemy, had so recently been their saviours. This misapprehension then current among the population enhanced their view that, although victors in the war, they had become victims of the peace.

For the Easter holidays the student was invited again to stay at his aunt's. At his earlier visit he had encountered another guest: a tense, nervous Norwegian girl. Her hosts did their utmost to put her at ease, as her exaggerated though genuine deference towards them was plainly discomforting. Unsurprisingly, the two nervous visitors turned to each other for support. The liaison was not discouraged although both were so discreet they were astonished (the young always are) that their mutual attraction was noticed. To their further amazement it was suggested that they hitch-hike for the holidays through southwest England. A memory would remain of a view of Bristol as they clung to barrels on the back of a cider lorry. Old terraced houses were strung in seemingly endless strings, but here, like beads in a necklace were draped over hills perched above the city. Their inhabitants walked down to work, he learnt, largely in tobacco and chocolate factories. Appropriately, the district was called Totterdown.

When he returned to college for the last term before the long summer vacation, his father's ever-enterprising secretary suggested that they write to all the Parisian couturiers asking for work experience before returning for the next college year. Such posts being much sought after, only one offer was received. This was from a house within the second rank and not among the 12 prestigious names. Nonetheless, the offer was gratefully accepted and so he set off.

Every railway station and each railway journey presented a parody on the theme of grime. It seemed people had laboured valiantly to paint on as much as they could. Decades of cobwebs dangled in festoons, held together with grease and filth. With some charity one could say it was not possible to imagine this world before the advent of steam cleaning. Charity too could have prompted the observer to remember the grime was the result of 200 years of industrial might. Soon, too, he heard the expression 'Where there's muck there's brass.' The all-pervading dirt seemed to show that the railwaymen were demoralised. They lacked leadership and ran the service as 'their' railway first and for the country second. Rail and some road transport had been nationalised as part of bedrock Labour government policy. Their manifesto, already in large part implemented, demanded public ownership of 'manufacture, distribution and exchange'. But just to show that things are not always quite what they seem, many rail companies had already been in financial trouble before the war, owing to the depression, and had lobbied the government to take them over. Pro-public or pro-private majority sentiment tends to fluctuate down the years when ownership of utilities is in question.

The carriages were shunted onto the cross-channel ferry, to be hauled by a French locomotive on arrival. The French railways, although state-owned, were much superior and as an institution an object of national pride. They were said to have saved the nation when the whole country lay under heavy snow in the winter following the war. The adage that 'it is better to travel than to arrive' aptly describes the sinking feeling experienced by those who (unlike a small minority), do not feel a sense of elation on finding themselves in a strange city speaking a strange language. Guarded optimism regarding his schoolroom French was soon dispelled in the cruelest fashion. He had been told accommodation could be found at Cité Université. This was reasonably central, but pronunciation was his downfall as everyone he encountered (with expansive gestures indicating considerable distance) pointed ever eastward. All these worthies understood him to mean Cité Universit*aire*, which proved to be a gigantic sprawling campus in a far suburb. Worse, it was closed and was not offering accommodation during the vacation.

It was very hot and he carried two suitcases. Backpacks were almost unknown and that simple, marvelous invention, wheels on a frame for a suitcase, was still more than a decade away. Unable to retrace his steps, he eventually staggered into the cheapest of hotels and, hyperventilating, suffered the only asthma attack he was ever to have.

The next morning he presented himself at the couturiers. It was plain that his allowance would stretch to about three nights' accommodation at a hotel, leaving nothing for food. Somehow he had to find lodgings. Luckily, the couturier's wife, who was also *directrice* of the house's *salon*, had engaged a 17-year-old girl as a *débutante*, or trainee in reception.

Ariane, a pretty redhead, had so much talent that she went on to run two of the top couturiers' salons. Never lacking in the requisite charm for greeting clients, neither would she quail before the most arrogant. Her innate aplomb (or *chutzpah*, as she was a Polish Jew), lifted the spirits of the anxious supplicant, and more so when she offered him board at her mother's flat. So at the end of the day he accompanied the girl to her home. The route they followed (usually by foot for lack of the fare) displayed more French material culture than any similar three-mile walk in France. From the Arc de Triomphe and Champs-Elysées, Palais, Tuileries Gardens and Palace Louvre, to their destination at Les Halles they passed monuments beginning in the early 19th and ending at the 11th centuries. Ariane's mother's flat overlooked Les Halles market, in constant use for 1500 years.

Madame's small top-storey flat was one floor of a building of much earlier vintage than those of the seventeenth to nineteenth centuries which dominate so much of Paris. Yet it was of the same height and so shared in the designed uniformity which as it is blended with elegance gives to Paris its confident air. In that city even dilapidation is dignified, not squalid. As to his hostess, a nice side of youth is that the young seldom make comparisons of people's circumstances as they have neither time nor cause to evaluate them. As with her daughter, Madame had a strong character and confronted hardship without a murmur. Piece-work sewing of cheap clothing was her lot, a situation that no doubt arose because her best friend had run off to Mexico with her husband. As for the lodger, he was in his usual familiar situation – in an unfamiliar place – and busied himself designing clothes in the hope of pleasing the couturier.

The couturier, a Hungarian Jew whose mother tongue was German, had a small but loyal following in tailored suits. He provided his new recruit with plenty of work of a repetitive and simple nature. Weeks went by and the assistant became increasingly concerned that he was learning next to nothing. He hoped that things might improve, and twice asked his employer for more interesting work. The response was a curt "*Non*", and that was contrary to the spirit of his unpaid work-experience (*stagiare*) post. The date was fast approaching for his return to London and the new term. Equally depressing was the thought of rejoining the student body, among whom he had somehow failed to make friends. The cream-painted concrete walls of his YMCA room resembled a prison cell. Returning to the company of the cell-mate stretched out on his bunk like a consumptive held little allure. This last prospect convinced him to persuade his father via his 'stepmother' (a title she had graciously accepted) to let him remain in Paris in the hope of better things.

Any foreigner at the time could not fail to remark on or be affected by the people's mood. In contrast to the jollier materialism of later decades in Europe, the pervading moroseness was palpable. If the British were sullen, the French were sour. Any man in the street could assess their relative situations. Britain's debt was much greater, for the French with their Vichy wartime government had managed to retain their gold (in Martinique) to underpin their currency. Britain's withdrawal from Empire was orderly, in contrast with the French experience: in 1954 France, after bitter fighting, had failed to hold Indochina, and now four years on was still struggling to keep Algeria. In 1956 there had been the humiliation for both Britain and France as allies in an attempt to regain control of the recently nationalised Suez Canal. Further dejection followed as Krushchev exploited this distraction to crush the Hungarian rebellion. The Cold War intensified once again as Krushchev removed his shoe at the UN and hit the lectern, shouting, "We will bury you!" It was chastening to recall that prior to Stalin's death in 1953 Krushchev had been his henchman, and Stalin had expressed regret that following the fall of Berlin he had not ordered the Red Army to take Paris as well.

Together with these sober distractions Parisians were morose on a personal and national level as they had to contend with the legacy of wartime occupation. Those who had legitimately and understandably co-operated with the occupying Germans (sanctioned by their own Vichy government) remained at every level in positions of authority. Those who had actively or passively resisted and refrained from profiting from the situation resented this. Classically, this created a climate that with Germany's defeat could only be tempered by a long passage of time. For the moment there was no gaiety and his fellow workers made plain to the young hopeful that theirs was a *vie de cochon* confined by commuting, work and sleep: *metro–boulot–dodo*.

Suddenly these tensions found release on the streets. The dignity of the Fourth Republic was affronted by the unauthorised action of the army, which deployed paratroops ostensibly to support the government. It became plain after a polite delay that the army intended to stiffen the resolve of those who were wavering in their desire to keep Algeria French. One background to this display was the frequent machine-gun battles between rival Algerian independence factions who were contesting the sole right to treat with the French government. Although the political Right wing sought support from the army, the latter was cautious as almost half of the French electorate had, since the war, and earlier, voted Communist. The stand-off in the streets persisted for some weeks and descended into farce when a champion of the Right and Algeria for the French, Jacques Soustelle, smuggled himself into the Elysée Palace in the hope of influencing the President. He arrived in the boot of an official car.

Farce notwithstanding, the Parisians continued glumly to go about their business. The Left would not yield to the Right and the army deemed it imprudent to enforce a change in policy. In a nation renowned for its political and ideological intransigence, the Left was formidable. The leading intellectual Jean-Paul Sartre remained an avowed Communist, quite unswayed by the Soviets' crushing of Hungary two years earlier. In these circumstances a rightist coup supported by the army could not gain traction in mainland France, and so the Right resorted to rebellion with the army in Algeria, and this was successful.

With this result the Right was able to influence events and soon a general consensus brought forth the man that (in extremis) was acceptable, provided that his own terms for the acceptance of the presidency were confirmed by plebiscite.

His terms demanded a new constitution in order to avoid the constant political regroupings and changes in government, thus ending the Fourth Republic.

In addition, there was such a severe devaluation that middle-aged and older people continued to refer to the currency for decades by its original name. (One franc became one centime!) Lastly, of greatest consequence for the moment; he pledged that Algeria would remain French.

The campaign for the presidency was an impressive affair. General de Gaulle employed a tactic that through circumstance he had been able to call his very own. As leader of the Free French forces, he had been sensibly permitted by the Allies to enter Paris in the vanguard for its liberation in 1944. The general's method, both dramatic and theatrical, was *le bain de foule* – to bathe in the crowd (as saviour). He had then become President and two years later resigned in disgust. Now, 12 years on, an exceptionally tall man, he strode once more among the crowd who in adulation clamoured, "De Gaulle! De Gaulle! De Gaulle!" As the campaign for his installation continued motorists thumped their horns with five beats: 'Al-ger-ie-Fran-caise!" He came to power on the promise that it would remain French and then gradually and skillfully abandoned his supporters as by stages he negotiated that country's independence. De Gaulle reigned for ten years and then retired (on his own terms) in 1968 owing to the rebellion against conformity that swept western countries in the late 1960s.

Bemused by these events, the lodger watched as his landlady too shouted from her window, "De Gaulle! De Gaulle!" Odours of fruit and vegetables floated upwards as the millennia-old market was swept clear for another day. Semi-resident *clochards* (tramps, who in France are an institution rather than a problem) scavenged and at night lit fires heaped with fruit-crates, got drunk, fought, and fell asleep under heaps of sacks. After two months it was time to move on. Ariane was expecting a visit from her lover, an English actor twice her age; the French say another language is best learnt on the pillow, and indeed her English was more than adequate. Ariane's mother arranged for the lodger to board with her seamstress. No doubt Madame was glad to see the back of him. His French was so bad and his spirits so low she deserved sympathy. The French abhor heaviness, phlegm and silence. He overheard Madame say to her daughter, "He must have been beaten as a child." Well, he did feel like a beaten cur.

The seamstress's apartment was more spacious. Perhaps there had been a better outcome after the defection of the husband. Her daughter was, in contrast to Ariane, sulfurous, pouting, idle, and grubby. The newcomer had only just enough sophistication to foresee a possibility of entrapment: the girl sidled passed the furniture with the lubricity of a cat on heat. Secluded inside the entrance to the building were two professionals (one heavily pregnant) of a sunnier disposition. He was obliged to pass between them on entering and leaving. There was a cheery rivalry evident: they plainly were confident he would require their services sooner rather than later. How mistaken they were!

Not only was he devoid of libidinous intent, but he had no money and was too embarrassed and ashamed to ask for more. (Madame had complained of the lack of profit from his board.) The flat was dirty (the seamstress's way of washing linen was to soak things in the bath and then let them drain from a stick for days.) It was imperative that he should find somewhere else to live, and look for a better job.

In overviews of the past, hindsight may receive too much credit. Surely despite his youth he could not have been oblivious to the evident wealth of many? The explanation was simple: the ever-threatening Left in France had not come to power. Result: austerity and crippling tax in Britain; in France, things much as they had been pre-war. With *Schadenfreude* the French relished the standing joke about the English: that when they came to Paris all they could afford was an omelette and a glass of water. The English were obliged to *rire jaune* (wear a sickly grin in adversity). The dozen top houses of haute couture, in addition to their home support, enjoyed patronage from South America, which was in the grip of embezzling right-wing dictatorships. North Americans had not yet arrived in large numbers.

Ariane wrote out a sequence of phrases in French that just might assist him as he knocked on salon doors. He had to hope that the 'exchange' of conversation would run as planned, and that the reply to his rote-learned phrases would elicit a positive response. Although he went from door to door his interviews could be described as restoring the phrase 'a dialogue of the deaf' to its original meaning. Despite this, however, a degree of accuracy was achieved in that the response was always in the negative. The 'nothing ventured, nothing gained' formula was truly put to the test.

These exercises took place over a series of Saturday mornings, to the displeasure of the couturier who regretted that the stupid *goy* would not be turning up just then for another period of unpaid slavery. Yet the man had his problems. His relationship with his wife was brittle. It had declined to the level of mercenary, or the *interessé* (the French, in their frankness, are not adept, or see no need to conceal these matters). This being the case, the man fell increasingly prey to his suspicions, well-founded or not. He would gently lift the phone and listen in to his wife's conversations in reception. Meanwhile the assistant found that his working prospects showed no improvement and it was essential to find somewhere else to live.

Through an advertisement a chance arose to share a dilapidated flat with an old lady in the smart 16th *arrondissement*. Madame Bobrikoff was hunchbacked and seemed older than her 72 years. She had long been a widow and like thousands of other *emigrés* in Paris had fled the Russian Revolution in 1917. Her husband, a cavalry officer, had joined the French army to continue the struggle against the

Germans. Having fought with distinction he was embraced by the saviour of France, Marshall Foch, and received the Légion d'Honneur.

Although pleasant and uncomplaining, Madame could not help but make evident her lack of any further interest in life. All her meager possessions were bundled up in small parcels of paper and string and set neatly about the room. She had no relatives, nor indeed any connections or visitors, so she had arranged matters to cause strangers as little trouble as possible. One saucepan sufficed for her to heat a little milk or soup in the tiny kitchen she was obliged to share with a run-of-the-mill young man. 'Obliged', of course as always everywhere, politicians had failed to adjust a war widow's pension for inflation. Madame held no rancour against the Soviets and felt on balance that the Russian people enjoyed a better life under their regime. She believed too that the USSR was permanent (it endured another 35 years).

His bedroom enjoyed a view ideal for distracting those who suffer endless anxiety. It looked out upon a schoolyard of the very young at play. This prospect of trees, sun, shadow and joyful shrieks was everything in perfection save in one respect. Madame constantly threw bread onto the roof adjoining, just under the kitchen window. Short in stature, she could not see over the sill. Along with that balm to the soul of all old ladies, pigeons, were rats. He was astonished to see that the birds were without fear and would beat the rats away with their wings. Soon there were rats galore. Lifting the lid of an empty dustbin in the basement, he found several. It was just beyond their capability to leap out as the bin's sides were metal and shiny. Luckily, his Vietnamese friend came by and killed them. But the bread-throwing continued. Pigeons and old ladies are a formidable combination.

Doky Thai was the victim of a shocking French Government fraud. Before French Indochina fell to the Communists his father had lodged funds in France for his son's education in medicine. On his arrival the authorities denied all knowledge of it. A quiet but resolute man, Doky was determined to support himself one way or another to become a doctor. He learnt to play the guitar and, with his girlfriend, who sang, they played by night at restaurant tables. Thai's girl Greta was tall, very blond and Danish, while he was brown, slight and short. For the times, such a pairing was unconventional, even startling. Regrettably, they overheard the occasional lewd aside.

The would-be couturier's lodgings were more congenial, but he had little money left for food. Luckily, the summer of 1959 was long and hot, and resulted in a glut of excellent tomatoes on sale for next to nothing. These with bread were his diet for some weeks and soon he had to buy braces to keep his trousers up. Following which, owing to diminished resistance, he contracted and could not shake off a sore throat. Swallowing was painful. His employer noticed his assistant was wilting and to remake him fit for purpose bought him pills. There was no improvement and so the man inquired, with amazing gestures, as to whether he was taking them in the correct fashion. This procedure, unheard of in his experience, proved effective. In addition, to further his rehabilitation the couturier now gave him lunch in his splendid apartment (although the chill between husband and wife did restrict his appetite). A parcel too arrived by post at his lodgings: a round cheese and some yeast extract. On a visit to Paris his stepmother had seen his condition and asked his father to increase his allowance. He replied, "If he is hungry send him a food parcel." A little later his stepmother did prevail and he received a small increase. It was all very awkward: he sympathised with his father's point of view as a self-made man, but on the other hand he had not intended (though indeed he was invited) to be a supplicant.

Being allocated an allowance was one thing, but actually receiving it was another. He established with certainty that his money was telexed from an English bank without fail fortnightly. With a cynicism to make any mendicant gasp the French bank would deny all knowledge of it. Having traipsed across Paris, cap in hand, he frequently received a cold and surly *"Non, Monsieur."* Remonstrating in fractured French only added to his humiliation. The bank was simply 'making a turn': playing with his and others' money over the weekend on the world's exchanges as they opened and closed through the time zones. So he was obliged to repeat the long walk, which encouraged him to indulge in some speculation about the French mindset. It seemed that they felt honour-bound to take advantage of anyone in a vulnerable situation. Generally, it appeared they thought the person concerned was in a predicament because they had acted foolishly, and so on their part it would be stupid not to profit by it. In dealings with each other the French were formally polite, not naturally polite. It was finally some small consolation to find they could be almost as rude to each other as to a foreigner.

Something had to be done about his situation. The tasks he performed were so menial he could not by any stretch of the imagination pretend he was learning anything. His excellent stepmother arranged translation of another letter in search of a new position. And one, almost too good to be true, was offered – with the pre-eminent house of Christian Dior. Dior himself had died some years earlier, but the house still basked in his world-wide reputation as creator of the post-war New Look. At long last Marcel Boussac, who owned the house as part of his textile empire, had appointed a successor: Dior's 20-year-old protégé, Yves Saint Laurent. The daring choice of one so young stimulated the press the world over as Paris was then, and more than ever since the arbiter of fashion.

So our young man was cautiously optimistic. After all, the house had replied on the basis of his request for a place as a *stagiare modéliste* which by definition meant there would be opportunities to learn and assist in design. 'Modelling on the stand' (draping toile on a dress-stand to achieve a design) interested him greatly. In anticipation he was humility itself (it was not as if he had come to Italy to teach the Italians how to cook spaghetti.) So the great day arrived and he presented himself as directed and was ushered into a huge *atelier* (workroom). About 70 women and girls were seated at seven long tables, making tailored costumes by hand but with a few machines for the longer seams. At the end of the room, seated either end of a raised platform, a man and a woman sat in grim silence with scarcely any other function beyond surveying the timid assembly. Prison warders watching a work detail would have looked more kindly upon their charges.

The connotations of the scene are assembled in retrospect but are convincing as to the climate of the time. The Boussac empire was a pre-war and wartime conglomerate akin to the great German industrial cartels. It was in service to Vichy France and the German war effort under the terms of Marshall Pétain's compromise with Hitler. Pétain promoted his devotion to France in authoritarian terms, much as Hitler did in Germany. Vichy France – clerics and the wealthier Right wing of old money – felt that de Gaulle had treated Pétain (the hero of Verdun) harshly. Pétain's rallying call to France after the defeat ("*Travail! Famille! Patrie!*") has the same clamour of authoritarian purpose as the German "*Ein Volk! Ein Reich! Ein Fuhrer!*"

It was plain that, placed among the workers as one of only two males in the atelier, he would be expected to sew. Of course he made no complaint (sewing being a useful skill for any couturier) and remained expectant that, as outlined in their letter, they would invite him to view or assist in design. As the days ran into weeks, and although his work was thought satisfactory, no invitation was forthcoming. Worse; the *surveillante* – the female 'guard' of the two on the platform – let it be known (intentionally in his hearing) that "whether he turns up to work or not is of no consequence to us." This observation was the legacy of a regime in France that was accustomed to coercion and abuse of its workforce. All the girls were unhappy and bemoaned their *vie de cochon*. (Such a legacy persisted in the police and it was not until many years later that younger policemen who had not served under Vichy, and so had not the same loyalty, ensured the underlying Fascist police culture was fully exposed. Among the shameful actions of the Parisian police was an incident known as La rafle du Vel d' Hiv in which they willingly helped the Germans to round up the city's Jews before they were transported to the gas chambers. The identity of those responsible was not made known to the public until the seventies.)

An inducement to the girls was a canteen. Being without funds, he was even ignorant of its location. He persisted in telling them he was not hungry. Any bread he could have brought would have disclosed the depth of his impoverishment. He missed out on the couturier's lunches that had kept him well nourished and he lost weight again. In those days French workers did not enjoy *la pause* (a tea break) and working solidly from 8 till 12 saw their nation through many a crisis. (In London many were trundling into work at 10.) One day in the *atelier* the workforce were 'requested' to give blood. All lined up to receive the blood group test of a prick before the thumb nail. As the sole male he went to the front of the queue. The prick barely felt, he glanced down to see two spots like black treacle struggling to show. Sinking to the floor, he revived in time to see that, fearing the worst, three of the girls had also fainted. Much embarrassed, he insisted that the medics try again, but twice more on attempting to give blood he fainted and so was sent on his way.

In his condition it was inadvisable to be playing rugby, but as youth must have an outlet, he turned out for the lowest-ranked team of a smartish club. Invariably such teams do not train, being composed of players who know that their elevation to a better team is unlikely. Harmless on the face of it, the reality is rather different. Unfit players blow up and get angry, blaming everyone but themselves for their inability to keep up with the play. Just as bad are the lowest-ranked referees who lack the ability to discipline such players and are even intimidated by them. Finally, and absurdly, both referees and players can be ignorant of the rules, sometimes with serious consequences.

Such information, of little interest to most, was the background to his everlasting if mild disfigurement. Within the first minute of play, the ball having gone into touch, the opposing players lined up to jump for the ball at the throw-in. Ignorant of the rules, his opposite number encircled him with his arms in a tight grasp to prevent him from jumping. To break the hold he swung his arms down firmly, though without intent to injure … and then regained consciousness stretched out on a table in the changing rooms. He learnt later that the player had knocked him unconscious with a blow to the jaw, and as he lay on the ground had kicked his head. Luckily the boot had struck his mouth and not his eye or temple. An inch-long gash had been opened on the top lip. The doctor advised against anaesthetic as this would make the wound too stiff to sew neatly. So he lay on his back, watching the needle and thread going up and down. Surprisingly the operation was not too painful as the flesh was indeed numb. As to the significance of the incident, the French do not have a tradition of team games. *Le fair play* is merely an add-on rule of the particular team game in question. For them adherence to fair play is not innate. Their concept of chivalry – *Messieurs les Anglais tirez les premiers* '– (Englishmen, please shoot first!) has little to do with fair play!

All in all, things were going swooningly if not swimmingly. The ongoing experience at Dior was depressing since he was simply helping to assemble an off-the-peg range of suits whereas he had been led to believe that there would be some encouragement for his hopes. *Chez* Mme Bobrikoff there were problems too. The girl from Norway had found a position as an au pair in Paris as part of her education, and naturally enough they resumed their relationship. Such being the folly of youth, this did not improve the French of either. His error was the greater, as his girl was anything but fluent in English and frequent failure on her part to understand the idiom caused her to fly into a towering, tearful rage. Calming the poor girl and explaining that she had misunderstood took much of his time. Plainly he was teaching her English when he should have been improving his French. Luckily, Mme Bobrikoff was sympathetic. She no doubt found the drama diverting.

Our innocent was ensnared by a situation that was depressing to recall, onerous to record, and debilitating to read. For those reflecting on a grim time the correction due is to remember that retrospect and hindsight lead to unhappy recollection. Final assessments can make a bad situation worse or a good one better. He felt he was but a passive observer, conscious enough to be prey to anxiety but unable to act.

He heard that the London Society of Couturiers was to hold a fashion show in Paris. Naturally, this was of as much interest to the French as English cooking and it was difficult to find mention of it in the newspapers. Nevertheless they rented the beautiful Hotel Crillon for the venue and asked for volunteer dressers to assist the models to change rapidly before each sally up the catwalk. The ever-hopeful obliged, and after the show approached a couturier for a job

in London. "Would there be an opportunity to assist in design?" he asked, inevitably. An unequivocal "Yes" was the response. With raised hopes he made preparations to leave. Apart from a lack of progress in his work, the sojourn in Paris had been so grim that even to escape would be a triumph. Sentiment against the Anglo-Saxons was at its height as the French endeavored to free themselves from their recent wartime humiliation. Happy to welcome NATO headquarters to Paris at the height of the Cold War (the Cuban missile crisis was approaching), de Gaulle swiftly expelled the organisation (and later quit it altogether) after the French developed their own nuclear deterrent. The despicable English gutter press responded readily to the ill-feeling and sold millions of newspapers over decades on the theme that "They will never forgive us for having saved them!" The French, better educated and with scarcely any yellow press, were enhanced through their disdain of such sentiments.

Taking care to ask at Dior for a cynical piece of paper (which of course did not state that unwittingly he had been pressed into their chain gang), he said goodbye to the girls. Stepping outside, he reflected that although the star was within the building he had never, even at a distance, set eyes on the shining Yves Saint Laurent. (For some years his kind-hearted stepmother, on business and visits to her lovers, called on Madam Bobrikoff until one day she found that the old lady had been tidied away together with her bundles of paper and string.) With a sense of relief bordering on elation, he arrived back in London. Now surely there would be no unfair impediments to his progress. His good fairy stepmother had found him a spacious room on one of London's few hills and he attended upon his couturier-saviour without delay.

It is only the daily drip of accumulating disappointment that eventually depresses all hope. Ushered once more into a workroom to sew did not automatically compromise his prospects. And assembling another's creations is of value, until one must accept stark reality that things will go no further. At least he was paid; even a pittance was an improvement. A remedy to his problem might lie in attaining proficiency at pattern-draughting so he enrolled at night school. Compared with Dior the enterprise was tiny: about eight workers on one floor making bespoke suits and similar on another making dresses. There was an congenial, almost too undisciplined atmosphere which was quite striking, remembering the cowering workers at Dior. This being the case, each individual had an identity and therefore a personality.

The workroom was never silent unless there was a rush on to meet a deadline. It was a perfect forum for banter. Prosperity, relative to the austerity most people had known, was at hand; sufficient for the prime minister to announce electorally that "You've never had it so good!" One seamstress with a husband, a car salesman, was particularly pleased with her lot. Now indeed there were cars to sell – and no longer restricted for export. With a council flat and subsidised cheap rent in the centre of London, her disposable income gave her cause to feel superior. Her workmates were constantly reminded that she only turned up for 'pin money'. Neither was this an idle boast: husband Alec had taken her on holiday to the south of France, and they would be going again. Her colleagues felt this couldn't be soon enough, as plainly they were more use to her as an audience than her pin-money wages. Her next trip did not eventuate. Alec was paralysed with a stroke so there was no more mention of pin money. The poor woman now frequently broke down at work and her workmates genuinely felt her pain.

Unsurprisingly, present in the workroom was a woman whose character was in complete contrast. Rigorous and principled in every respect, yet by no means priggish, her total lack of humour mattered not at all. Her inner strength too was manifest outwardly: regardless of the weather she always wore a cotton print frock. Always high in colour, Daisy plainly suffered from a continuous hot flush. Our innocent was tempted to seek piecework for better pay as a felling hand (slip-stitching lining into clothes), to which Daisy responded with "I wouldn't think much of you if you did." Tailoring and the rag trade were largely a Jewish and East End tradition, and it was common for some exponents to work too in the West's Mayfair, at the expensive end of the trade. This workroom's amiable example plied a rapid needle and oozed business acumen. Assisted by his indefatigable sunny nature, he steadfastly refused to pay any shopkeeper's ticket price for goods on principle. The company was further graced with a young and pretty cockney lass who each day swooned with concupiscent delight as she reflected on the night before. Reticently presiding over the assembled was the head tailor, whose deference towards the couturier seemed excessive to someone from a country with a tradition that Jack was as good as his master. The couturier himself appeared most days after lunch and paced the room belching as he measured a lordly pace among his workers. His Canadian wife, who was considerably older, directed the enterprise and seemed most unhappy. What of the observer? He was careful to be careful but was perhaps not careful enough (antipodean habits die hard.) On one occasion the head tailor said, "Now that's *just* what I thought you would say."

Meanwhile the Norwegian girlfriend had left Paris and found work as assistant to the owner of a London art gallery which was well known for launching artists who later became famous. Although she was academically untutored, her dedication to art was so genuine and convincing that she remained wedded to pictures for life. She was tall and slender with graceful poise, and her reverence when confronted with the mysteries of art was sincere. At this point the good fairy stepmother reappeared and ordained in her infinite kindness that the young couple should have somewhere they could call 'home' together. Flats were scarcer than hen's teeth but with her boundless ability she soon found one: a Victorian red-brick London mansion flat, spacious and with high ceilings. It was well it was unconfining, as having paid the rent they had hardly the means to step outside the door. This was inconvenient as his girl's Paris rages continued and it would have been useful to escape her violence. Ever demure at work, she was the reverse at home.

With prospects at work so bleak there seemed no hope that he would enjoy the traditional haute couture methods of creating a style, then fitting and displaying the result on a model. The alternative for remaining with fashion could only be to enter the less-expensive end of the trade. Accurate pattern-draughting together with appropriate design are essentials for success, so he attended night school. In time he hoped he would become sufficiently proficient, and finding a new position he gave notice to the dissembling and flatulent couturier.

The contrast between the world of haute couture and the savagery of the raw rag trade is unimaginable. In times when women were still regarded as second-class citizens in the workplace the situation was quite otherwise in the garment industry. The American owners of the Wendy Dress Company opined that their manageress could run a building site in New York. Placed within a glassed-in room on a huge shop floor, rows of machinists and cutters awaited the newcomer's designs and patterns of a 'snappy number'. This currently was to be of satin and bright acid boiled-sweet colours. With a life-or-death anxiety to please, he exceeded the limits of the mixture of the dress which was to be mass-produced. "Look," said his colleague, "You've put *four* separate designs into the one dress!" There was no system of tweaking and adjusting as in couture: the design was immediately draughted to a pattern and the material cut to stock sizes.

He was soon dismissed, and the matter-of-fact way in which it was done should have taught him not to take it to heart. But this was not yet the carefree sixties: conformity in comportment was still the norm; rejection was rejection. Next, in the grimmest part of the East End his natural inclination towards couture design led him to present a dress too refined for that section of the trade. A fellow designer told him forcibly that his offering was 'gormless', and ever after he regretted not punching the fellow. Sacked again, he found work in the West End, where he felt that his novel design would be accepted. It passed muster, but he was increasingly nervous and could not follow it with another. Anxiety does not assist the free spirit of creation, and he was shown the door once more. Thus is natural self-esteem and vanity corroded by the acid of humiliation and fear.

Fear too, flashed across the face of his next employer – a face reconstructed following a wartime Spitfire crash. He had been drawn through sufficient means to the glamour of fashion, but his fear was evident as he saw his good money being thrown after bad. Emotionally dominated by his brash sales manager, he was constantly told that the business needed more money when in fact it just needed more sales. The firm's highly competent designer had found a better job and given notice. The newcomer was to replace him, and if he could stop trembling, the prospects were good. Specialising in the medium-to-better end of the trade in woollen suits, he had an immediate success: his double-breasted design was displayed in the smartest of Knightsbridge windows. The chief designer duly left and he was on his own. Not for long. The garments were made by an outworking firm who carried responsibility alone for manufacture. Its owner visited and announced that he could not have confidence in cutting cloth to the new man's patterns.

Lacking now any stomach to test the job market further, his only alternative was to attempt something alone. Designers are well paid in fashion and at least at each dismissal he had been paid and had accumulated more money than ever before in his life. Why not try to exploit the design of the only commercial success he had had, and use it to seek further work?

At about this point suddenly the sixties arrived. Fashion and the rag trade saw changes that sociologists will mull over forever. London's high streets, helped by a complicit media, inaugurated the 'swinging sixties' look and every corner of the world took notice. Paris, hitherto followed slavishly, was suddenly obliged to look at London. Young designers appeared who had never been influenced by Paris or haute couture. One, a young woman his own age, was more prominent than the others and surrounded by top-flight businessmen determined to exploit her capabilities. The forcibly self-employed hopeful decided to visit her. His plan was to sell a design and a production run undertaken on his own responsibility at an agreed price. He knew that she would want tighter sleeves as a fashion statement for a younger market, and indeed she liked his sample – as long he agreed to give it closer-fitting sleeves. He duly presented the altered sample, but no: she wanted them (dangerously) tighter still. She would accept the 40 or so suits if this were done. They were now too tight.

Possibly a more experienced operator would have simply delivered the order unaltered, as final steam-pressing will shrink wool. With a half-embarrassed wintry smile the woman rejected the 40 suits. When he protested, her male sponsor merely responded with silence and one raised upper-crust eyebrow. As with the brand-new fashion scene, these people too were new and would not have wished to be associated in image with those who traditionally ran the rag trade. 'They' knew how to behave. Ruefully the entrepreneur calculated the extent of his loss. He reflected on the fable of Hansel and Gretel imprisoned in a cage for fattening by the blind witch. Cleverly, they pushed an old bone instead of an arm through the bars. Their arms would not fatten to become too fat for their sleeves, and so they survived.

The influence of this young woman designer eclipsed by far that of her contemporaries. A cosmetic range added further to her success and the media fawned. She was endlessly interviewed and even her speech patterns were imitated. Questioned on matters in general her comments were interlaced between phrases with the mutually explanatory "you know". In no time, 'you know', everyone was 'you know'. Such prominence warranted an autobiography, in which with unfeigned indelicacy she described the joy, excitement and freedom that the advent of the birth-control pill had brought her. She and her coterie had seized the moment and fashion in clothing was the essential for living in style. London's Carnaby Street, with dozens of fashion shops cheek-by-jowl, led the craze. Then after this phenomenon became assimilated as the norm, fashion trends in the seventies were led rather by clubs, celebrities and rock music.

After his bruising encounter with the high-street rag trade, couture regained its allure. He would design and make a 'collection'. He still had some savings with which to buy the finest woollen cloth for a tailored collection. His slender girlfriend would model the clothes before an invited audience at the very attractive venue of his aunt's Oxford residence. A couple of dozen people were politely encouraging and the *Oxford Mail* also attended. The result of just one order taken was a disaster to be recalled for ever more (it is sometimes difficult to accept that one's humiliation is only wounded vanity.) The problem lay in fitting. He could design and make to a stock-size block pattern but had never received instruction in the mysteries of fitting from those for whom he slaved. His aunt's coat was short in the 'back balance'. She was by nature kindly but forthright. He was mortified.

To receive clients, he redecorated the sitting room to act as a salon. Gloss battleship-grey painted walls, deep mauve ceiling-to-floor curtains and sea-green soft furnishings made an unusual statement, and he was made to promise not to repeat it anywhere else in the flat. There was little danger of that, as he had expended his savings. The prospect of eviction loomed: the rent was high for an address of sufficient dignity to receive young Chelsea matrons. Hurriedly he took a job as a builder's labourer with a large firm. He soon realised that such a remedy in that country (at least in those times) was unusual, whereas from whence he came that was not so at all. The baseness of his workmates was, to gloss over the matter, dispiriting. He lacked the maturity yet to appreciate that any great city must contain the best and worst of people. The nature of the work was at least appropriate to the workforce and also less sophisticated in method than man's first attempts at building in prehistory. They were required to underpin a small department store before it was extended. This involved crawling on hands and knees underneath the existing foundations with small wicker baskets and then returning with the excavated soil, thereby making room for new footings. The pay was at basic rates despite the danger: five shillings and threepence an hour, identical to the rate for a seagull on the wharf he had received four years earlier. This at least said something for the financial stability of the sterling-area countries at the time.

Despite the poor pay, in a few short weeks he had the rent money and could begin work on the orders he'd obtained. Any trade occupation was of course forbidden in the residential flats. A bedroom converted to a workroom was all too visible to patrolling porters outside, so he kept the curtains permanently drawn. A succession of seamstresses worked with him in the gloom, four in total, but one at a time as there was never sufficient work for two. In sequence: a charming, resolute, well-bred English girl; a frighteningly devious Iranian Zoroastrian (fire-worshipper); a girl from Antigua, just 16, with enviable self confidence; and lastly a French girl with a calm, sunny nature. None stayed very long; whether because his career was not taking wing or for other reasons he could not tell. He did not seek adventure with his girls or clients, for apart from the moral aspect there was crisis and misery enough. Loyally, despite their difficulties his girlfriend gave up her lunch hour at work to buy his materials.

Occasionally his father called to offer 'encouragement' in his daunting way. His young wife too accompanied him but was always subdued in his presence. His convictions regarding the path to success were simple: "If you are good enough people will not allow you to escape, they will pursue you anywhere; there will be no hiding place." His views on free, unrestricted markets would have made Milton Friedman blench. In pursuit of this excellence his father quite rightly advised the necessity for leisure and fitness through sport, and the self-discipline required to make time for these pursuits. His son could not manage this prescription, much to his detriment as regular rugby would have benefited him in every way. Sewing in the gloom did nothing for the muscle tone of a young person. Eventually his girlfriend observed that he had arms like her grandmother.

This did not deter her from arranging their marriage that summer in Norway. Her family had been much affected by the war and German occupation. Forced to flee on skis to Sweden with his family, her father had made his way to England and was killed flying with the Royal Air Force. An uncle too, was assassinated on his doorstep and so the mother was left to bring up two daughters with little family support. She had then remarried much later and was again widowed. As to the groom, aged 24 he felt totally disembodied and, as marrying participants sometimes do, saw himself as a walk-on actor in a play until placed suddenly centre-stage with the bride and facing the congregation with the Lutheran minister. Such sudden exposure dramatised his situation (although he was not uncompliant) and his tears flowed in floods. Use of a handkerchief would have drawn attention so he let things be.

Two weeks of honeymoon followed on the family's tiny island, about the size of a house. He was not disconcerted to learn that his bride's mother would be with them, hoping that she would restrain her daughter's temper. To his dismay they all but set about him physically, both haranguing him morning to night. The mother, with a Scandinavian attitude to marriage, gave their prospects together as "three years at the most". To escape, he took to rowing their boat as often as possible. Unfortunately, rowing is a two-handed occupation so he was unable to ward off dive-bombing attacks from a seagull breeding colony nearby. Seals occasionally surfaced and observed his predicament with interest.

On their return to London, his wife announced her intention to have a baby. This was quite in the natural order of things: as young marrieds with a nice flat, their (or particularly his) questionable prospects were no factor in the decision. Else, how can life go on? His career continued to drift. He seemed to be making wedding dresses when his intention had been to make tailored suits. This was not in any programme for an up-and-coming couturier. Fatally (leaving aside the question of competence), he had failed to play sport and so mix socially with rugby players and their girlfriends and wives who would have enabled him to question his situation and goals. Orders, too, might have eventuated. A rugby-playing friend of renown called to warn him that all work and no play makes Jack a dull boy. But he heeded not. On a beautiful spring day he might look out, but seldom go out. There were just enough gardens in the vicinity to sustain that ever-joyful family of birds, the tit-mouse. Almost all English garden birds had been introduced to his country save these which seemed the most remarkable.

Then, as matters drifted, an event as bewildering as it was unforeseen occurred. His father, though well-versed in the mantras and recipes of successful business, actually loathed it. His intention had always been to make money and get out. But emotionally embroiled in his own creation, he was incapable of negotiating its sale. He was mesmerised by the question as to whether he was asking too much or too little. Consumed with doubt, he lacked the calm approach to walk away (if only seemingly) from negotiations. Fortunately his young wife was all those things he was not, and she managed the sale perfectly. She then prevailed upon her husband to give his son a considerable amount of money on the basis that it is better to be gifted money when young rather than old when generally it is of less use. Embarrassed by the unexpected though welcome gift, he did not ask for details. Eventually he learnt the money was in US Treasury Bonds, to be held perhaps indefinitely, so it seemed irrelevant to his problems. The sum was not disclosed, nor the manner in which he might release the money, and he had no plans to inquire.

The matter however, burdened his father, who telephoned frequently to ask what he was doing about 'the problem'. His son was bemused: he knew nothing about any 'problem'. His father would not elaborate, concerned no doubt that his son would do something rash. Confusion reigned until the son learned independently what the problem was: were he to cash the bonds and remit the money to dollar-hungry Britain he would gain a premium, perhaps as much as 18 percent. Against that course of action was the possibility of an even greater devaluation after the money might have been prematurely repatriated. His father did not wish to see a large part of his hard-earned money lost in this way through an arbitrary and shameful devaluation imposed without warning overnight (as they always are, to avoid further speculation). So, fearing his son would repatriate the money (when he had no such intention), the father applied considerable pressure until his son suggested that he take the money back. Naturally this was not his wish and his son heard no more. Not long after, the pound (despite the usual tactical denials up to the last moment) was devalued. The disreputable statement of the prime minister is often quoted to illustrate the folly of restricting the international convertibility of a country's currency (exchange control). To a nation obliged to import most of its food he said, "The pound in your pocket tomorrow will be worth exactly the same as the pound in your pocket today."

These were still times without maternity leave whereby a mother with her newborn baby receives financial help by right from her employer or the state or both. Suddenly he saw that without his wife's salary they could not make ends meet. There seemed nothing for it but to confront the rag trade again with his talents. Lacking the stomach for another assault on London, he replied to an advertisement in the trade paper. The position offered was in Manchester, and travelling thither he was accepted. His new employer was of that stamp of gentleman who reaffirms faith during times of adversity that affect everyone. His successful business was what is known as 'vertically integrated' as all the garments made were sold exclusively through his own family's shops. Only the cloth was bought in. The design parameters were challenging, in that options for variety of design were limited as the business targeted the low-priced, middle-aged sector of ladies' fashion. The chance of selling many waisted overcoats to comfortably proportioned matrons was slim. Most coats were of necessity draped from the shoulders and sold on cloth, colour and just one design detail. It was more a tragedy than a mere disappointment that he did not see that in fact the test of a good designer is to succeed despite such limitations. Unaware of this, he found the design restriction confining. Embarrassingly, his kind and encouraging employer persisted in his belief that the newcomer could deliver.

Design was one thing, but once settled on a design, pattern-cutting was quite another. Rows of machinists awaited, lit by shafts of sunlight. Sunlight, as the factory was housed in a vast redundant cotton-spinning mill glazed throughout for maximum light to illuminate what had been giant looms. Manchester had long since lost that trade to India. In this venue of bright expectancy, somehow his clothes would not fit.

On Friday evenings he took the train to London, returning on Sundays. Door-to-door, with Sunday track maintenance the 160-mile journey took seven hours. Halfway the filthy British Rail train lurched to a stop at Crewe Junction for the long wait for another to clank onwards to the second-largest city in the realm. Such tribulation was as nothing compared with the weekend's sojourn with his wife. To what might later be described as a bipolar condition was added what also later became known as postnatal depression. The mere sight of her husband each weekend was a provocation. The woman foamed at the mouth with rage and used her wooden sandals on him like a meat cleaver.

The contrast with his employer was startling. Perhaps aware of his anxiety, he advised that he relax, not keep strict office hours, and wander about the city, the better to stimulate his muse. Such kindness of course increased the pressure: a faltering magician with failing tricks would have faced an audience with greater aplomb. Humiliation is increased with kind people because they wish you well. It was plain enough that he must be replaced. His employer asked him to remain and work with a replacement, and he would have done so but for the man's crushing goodwill.

Returned to London there was at least a pressing diversion from marital bliss. It would not have been a problem for his wife to care for the baby boy each day at the art gallery in relaxed, congenial surroundings. But the gallery was about to close. Its owner had advanced payments to her artists for too long on the prospects of future sales (and they repaid her by deserting to more prestigious galleries.) What was to be done? It seemed that he and the rag trade had examined each other at length and could not find grounds for another happy marriage. Recalling contentment he had known working on the land as a boy, it was just a short step to find a job through a farming magazine.

The position was offered for six months until one of the farmer's two sons returned from agricultural college. This seemed a sensible period of time to assess whether he could adjust to a farming life. He boarded with the farming family until his wife was able to join him to live in the cottage provided. Fifteen years had elapsed since he had worked on a dairy farm at the age of 12, and where a kind farmer had paid him well. In all that time there appeared to have been only one innovation: artificial insemination, so there were no bulls whereas earlier there were several. Productivity-boosting inventions such as portable electric fencing to ration pasture for the cows were unknown. Amazingly, no-one had yet invented a milking parlour with the cows in bails on a level higher than the man milking; and in consequence he stooped and crouched under each and every cow, morning and night. It was still not known that cattle are more averse to mild electric shock than humans, and the copious amounts of water thrown down to keep the floor clean increased the shocks the cows received. Some cows responded badly, making milking an arduous occupation.

The farmer's family forebears had held their land for 300 years. But farms are less static and settled than they appear. Boundaries expand or contract with farmers' fortunes and this farmer with his forward-looking sons was about to take over their neighbour. Quite possibly their ancestors had owned the neighbour's farm once, or equally this neighbour had owned them. His new employer had had difficult times and his hands trembled with anxiety. He was already at retirement age when he lost his entire shorthorn herd to tuberculosis, and now milked Friesians.

Installed in the farm's cottage with the baby boy, time hung heavily for the young wife, used as she was to the company of paintings and artists. Yet the Norwegians are a rural people who worship the outdoor life, and she looked the part, although her mood swings and violent temper continued. But there were greater concerns. Weeks of hard work and no wages. He hesitated to ask his employer. Memories of his Paris situation haunted him. The farmer's advertisement had said nothing of a 'trainee' position and he shrank from the thought of further upheaval (Up sticks? Where to? He had no transport: there was neither bus service nor telephone, nor neighbour within reach from whom to seek advice.) Added concern arose as there was doubt in his mind as to whether he was giving satisfaction to his employer. He could not drive, and the farmer, with poor sight, refrained entirely. Backing a tractor and trailer around farm buildings was almost beyond him. The farmer shook with suppressed rage as time and again the trailer locked up askew at right angles and jammed the alleyway.

In this situation, acute anxiety to please increased his panic. He rushed about making two trips to accomplish a task when one would suffice. The farmer, becoming angry, understandably accused him of not thinking. It seemed matters could not get worse, and on going home for breakfast after milking he locked himself in the lavatory and sobbed. Believing that the farmer was a righteous man was in the circumstances anything but a comfort as it put him squarely at fault. Each Sunday his employer attended church and it was gently made plain that the worker should attend with him and his family. He gladly complied.

Six weeks after his arrival the farmer handed him his wages at the full rate and up to date. Through this delay he identified himself as just another farmer who hated doing his books. Each morning after milking, his employer would unbend and relax a little with his herdsman. Amongst clouds of steam, their arms in hot water and suds, they washed the equipment. Invariably and unconsciously, their bucolic conversation betrayed each day their love for the land. For a moment the farmer's anxiety was put aside: the milk was in the churns and the ever-first-in-line bank manager paid until tomorrow. The herdsman of 30 years' service had, between milkings, an enviable winter occupation: the sublime and artistic job of hedge-laying. This worthy did not have to chase sheep about the farm in heavy gumboots. For the winter, sheep were brought all the way from Kent and each boarded for a shilling per week, while the cows stayed in their byres. The hedges were cattle-proof but not sheep-proof, and as the farm kept no dog he soon got fit for rugby. As he rushed about he reflected occasionally upon the historical curiosity that was close by in the hamlet. Its pub was named after the last man hanged in England for sheep-stealing. Cannard's grave was said to be beneath the pub's floor after, as the pub's sign made plain, he had swung there on a gibbet. A mile or so away lay the ancient sheep-dealing town of Shepton Mallet, one of a once-prominent few that with the medieval wool trade had given England its first real taste of wealth.

The farmer's son returned from college and a new position was found for the worker on a nearby farm. A handsome house was offered, which the young couple began to furnish before going on holiday. They now had a little car and their destination was his father's cottage by the sea. Confined for the long journey, the couple fought most of the way and he gripped the wheel tightly as the blows rained down. The harbour cottage's origins were as old as the church nearby, whose grounds held the grave of King Canute's daughter. The cottage was proof of the famous demonstration offered by the king to his subjects: it, like him, was unable to hold back the sea. The climate had changed, the sea level had risen, and now swans swam by at high tide, level with the window sill. To ensure that this charming aspect remained sustainable his father had had the room encased within with a metal tank.

The novelty of feeding swans at the window distracted the couple for a moment, but now they had full days for their quarreling which drowned out their baby's cries. Unwilling to endure the situation continually – at least not without a short break – on the third morning he went to London, informing his wife he would return the next day. A startled friend offered him his sitting-room couch and, refreshed, he returned in the morning only to find his wife and baby had gone. She had left no message. As they had not completed their move to the new farm he telephoned his ex-employer's farm. The farmer's wife confirmed sadly that she had come with the baby, gathered some things and taken the train to Newcastle. That could only mean that she had left by ferry for Norway.

There seemed no point in occupying the new farmer's cottage alone despite regret at inconveniencing him, nor in accepting the offer to board with the family. The prospect of such a closeted and regulated life was, even if beneficial, just too unappealing. Uninvolved in the drama and gamble of a farm's finances, he was merely a labourer and the repetitiousness of the work inclined him to see farms as factories without roofs. He had been taking an agricultural correspondence course, and an alternative would have been to go full-time to college. However, fate demanded a quick decision, and to the kind farmer's disappointment he chose not to join him. Suddenly he was no longer farming.

The money as bonds he had received from his father would have bought a viable farm (although unstocked and unequipped). Sophisticated joint farming ventures where one partner would provide the land and another working capital were not yet an option. This new situation had a liberating aspect. Perhaps it was because the witness to his rag-trade failures (although at least she had never reproached him for those) had fled across the waters and in one bound he was free. Why, he felt, should he abandon the sum of his strivings to adorn the fair sex? With so little success in designing and making clothes, could he not perhaps sell them? It was exciting to picture an array of tempting fashion assembled with the flair he did not doubt for a moment he possessed. Further, the premises where he would display these clothes would be unique. 'Shop' could not describe it; not even the newly coined term 'boutique' would suffice. He relished the idea of designing its interior. But where would all this take place? Not London he thought (too many grim memories): better to make a bigger splash in some smaller pond. But where? His employers shopped only in Bath, although it was no nearer than Bristol. This surprised him, as Bath was so much smaller and limited for choice. It was, they said because "in Bristol they'll steal the sugar out of your tea." Needless to say, the serious import of this observation was lost on him and he thought it merely quaint. He had at least been to that city for pig-rearing lectures but with his new project in mind obtained an introduction to an art-school lecturer through a rag-trade friend.

In the Second World War Bristol had been important for shipping and aircraft manufacturing and been quite heavily bombed. In consequence a vast new shopping precinct was built at some distance from the old city. By the early sixties streets of shops stood empty under equally un-let office blocks. They remained so for many years but what appeared to the unwitting observer as councillors' delusions of grandeur was tolerable enough for the property developers who could afford to bide their time. They paid no rates and the alternatives to placing their clients' money in this unedifying concrete were unattractive. The alternative was to invest in manufacturing but this was long before the advent of a certain woman, and industry suffered from constant strikes. In addition, inflation is always kind to established bricks and mortar, as building costs are increased by the risk of ever-greater inflation. So life-insurance pension-fund money in such development is a long-term investment and can afford to wait. As to the letting potential of the new shops, this was not helped by the repair and rebuilding of the old city. For a population of 300,000, widely dispersed, it was 'over-shopped'. A novel feature was its 200 pubs – many just the front rooms of street-fronted houses.

So, in the early sixties, Bristol, commercially dormant and residentially dispersed, slumbered. South Wales, to please a Labour-supporting electorate, had received a motorway years in advance of Bristol, for eventual connection to London. The prosperity that was to flow from that corridor was still 20 years away. The city contented itself with its long established light industries of tobacco, confectionery and semi-moribund aircraft manufacturing much dependent upon fickle government support. Nevertheless, Bristolians to a man were conscious of their city's proud past. They had no need of folklore to note the decay of their once-great merchants' houses. Endearingly, they knew their pre-eminent trade had been lost to Liverpool through their own complacency. Resting on their laurels, they slipped off their pedestal by failing to build new docks to receive the ever-increasing size and number of vessels.

He opted to lease a lock-up unit in the planners' unappealing concrete Utopia as the shops offered were of the right size and shape in which to create a contemporary art interior. The terms of the lease were attractive: 21 years with limited rent reviews at seven and 14 years. Inflation was running at six percent and seemed destined to go higher, so the rent would be amortised favourably in real terms. However, the later and still rare rates holiday was not offered by the council for new development. Increases year on year by this body, determined to target any commercial venturer – and with an inept zoning policy regarding rateable value relevant to street pedestrian flow – were the reality.

It appeared that his contact the art lecturer preferred the excitement and profit of transaction to art instruction. He excelled as a Mr Fixit, with contacts for everything and everybody. Not for a moment did he contemplate conventional shopfitters accustomed to fitting out look-alike interiors for chains. Avoiding them gave him much satisfaction. Practicing artists descended on the site – but at all hours. As artists through and through it was plain their habits were to be tolerated if anything was to happen. He almost camped in the place in order to let them in and out. Another curious feature emerged: they might announce at anytime that they had to "go and sign on". Bewildered, he had no idea that these people had registered as unemployed. He had never encountered unemployed people before. Slowly, it dawned on him that by implication he was complicit in defrauding the taxpayer in employing them even on a brief casual basis. Guiltily, he persisted with the arrangement; the superb art scheme was half completed.

This amounted to nothing less than the last word in contemporary movements: Optical or Op Art. Arguably more exciting than its predecessor (Popular or Pop Art, which creates kitsch in parodying comic strips with an air of superiority), Op Art gave welcome relief from that pretentious realism. His new devotees (even if their dedication to the movement might be fleeting) applied themselves with pleasure: after all, it was their own creation, painted at times of their own choosing and they were paid twice for it (once by the state). Except that they and others on site, including tradesmen, had an obligation to Mr Fixit as he had brought them there. It seemed too that they honoured this arrangement and Mr Fixit called in favours due in return as he wished.

Op Art, of simple forms and colours, once demonstrated as a startling novelty, had no further uses or applications. Red, green, and blue painted bands within a circle defied the eye's attempt to focus on the arrangement. This just danced about the wall. Spotlights reflected the mural on to white enameled steel tiles. A ceramic white tiled floor ensured equally that the art display remained the main focus. With a horror of the sameness of dress shops, whose clothes were always distributed around the walls, he determined on something different. He would have cabinets on wheels in the red, blue, and green Op Art colours. Mirrors, display mannequins, changing cubicles were art objects in themselves. With clothes chosen and orders placed there remained only the name to be decided upon. That was easy: with the Cold War and the new era of spy satellites, it had to be – in red, blue and green, and in neon – 'Orbit'.

The 'art object as shop' seemed in all respects just what he wanted: it was a dream come true. But this art-themed boutique gleamed with light in a concrete desert – people, he felt, must be made to know of it. Glossy *Queen* magazine might feature it, he felt, so he called on them in London with photographs. They agreed it merited placing in their editorial section, and sent photographers. He opened to trade and came slowly to sense that still chill known to shopkeepers condemned to wait. But for the moment he could animate the all-too-static solitary 'painting', his shop hung alone on the empty concrete parade. Movement in the window might be the answer. One of the artistic tribe who are forever their own masters created a life-sized puppet show. Two girls' figures were made and loosely jointed for a free dancing movement. They were then dressed and suspended together in a frame. Mechanical innovation was this artist's forté so he mounted and concealed an old washing-machine motor, attached a crank to its flywheel, and the two girls danced the day long.

Our innocent soon had cause to recall the farmer's warning that "They'll steal the sugar out of your tea." And equally, to learn why traditionally clothes in dress shops were seldom displayed in areas where the customer could not be seen. Arranged as they were about the floor space, the cabinets hid girls who could slip a dress from its hanger and into a bag unseen. Another dodge was to cover one dress on its hanger with a second and ask to try on the one visible. They then emerged, returning one dress as unsuitable to the assistant, having concealed the other while in the changing room. Three girls entering the shop at once with just one assistant to serve could be fatal. If one was adept at distraction the other two could cause havoc. At his first stocktake he was ashamed at his ineptitude and anxious about the consequences, as dozens of garments could not be accounted for. The shop looked sublime but the reality was grim. *Queen* magazine sent its results; in return for the editorial he had agreed to take 100 copies. The shop appeared just as he wished, but what could he do with them? Plainly they should be handed free one by one in the high street to passing girls. No doubt one or two were startled to be handed something for nothing without having to help themselves.

Cannot hindsight offer some excuse for this folly? Very little, save that market research was in its infancy. He was catering for young women who simply could not afford his clothes. A typist's wage in Bristol, as of course he learnt subsequently, was one-third that of her counterpart in London. The relatively few who were better off made a point of going 'up to town' – to London, more than a hundred miles distant – for their shopping. He was unaware of the depth of his predicament. A shop whose image shouted latest fashion could not 'trade down' by stocking cheaper clothes. This market was, in any case, well supplied. So he continued to throw good money after bad, making plain that to know the value of 'good' money it is best to make it oneself. Each week saw him well short of the break-even point for the business. Window-dressing, cleaning and trips to London and back to buy clothes in a day were all he could do to bring costs down. The suppliers in London were of that odious rag-trade ilk that he had so earnestly hoped never to set eyes on again. Although he paid cash on the nail, his small orders were treated with contempt.

That his shop's site was in a backwater was at least reflected favourably in the terms of his lease. Inflation, together with the likelihood that development would see neighbours appear in the empty shops, gave him encouragement. And it couldn't happen too soon! Time passed and the pedestrian flow did not improve. The dancing puppets in the window performed to an empty house and were chafing through their frocks. Was this a dance of death? Perhaps. With their electric current turned off they might have been mummies, or worse, two girls hanged for sheep-stealing.

There were few pedestrians and even a parked car was a welcome novelty: the occupants might discover the shop! Then, to his amazement, a full parking ban was imposed. There seemed no reason for it as there were no parked cars to obstruct the light traffic flow. It became obvious that the council, embarrassed by the lack of paying customers for its grandiose car-park building nearby, had decided to force cars into it. Then the rates went up. One showpiece dear to the councillors' hearts was the development of a students' union building for Bristol University. Bars, deep leather armchairs, a huge indoor swimming pool and pompous swathes of empty floor space rankled with shopkeepers who had to pay for it. He appealed against the rates, confident that the case in his favour was overwhelming. Foremost was the fact that the parade of new shop units had stood empty for some years. He, however, had obliged the council and it was plain that 'planner's blight' had not encouraged others to follow his example. Three ladies in flowered hats listened impassively and without comment to his case, then swiveled their heads as one to hear the valuation officer's reply. This was simply that the council had decided that his deserted backwater was integral to the high street around the corner and gloried in its title of Zone A! The officer's delivery and demeanour were hardly persuasive, even considering this arbitrary decision. But it was quite enough for these ladies, who dismissed his appeal without a qualm. Dumbfounded, he reeled back to his deserted shop, which was lit like a beacon in a desert. These were the days when women of a certain age had never been exposed to the rigours of career and the commercial life. It filled him with horror that these women believed they were honourably performing a civic duty rather than admitting they were there for the social cachet.

The next worst thing to having no customers is having to turn them away. It may stretch credibility, but this was the situation for a partnership of three gay boutique owners in the old part of the city. Apart from the flair and flamboyance that gays, with confidence and style, use to put customers at ease, these three had something else. They were selling to boys (youths if you must) whose wages were more than double that of girls and whose instincts were tribal. This induced them to focus on the identical 'must-have' object. It is that intense post-adolescent moment when only the 'right' clothes can put them at ease.

At its height, the queue to obtain this necessity stretched some 30 yards up the pavement from their small shop. Having viewed these events with astonishment and made the comparison with his own predicament, he approached the three gentlemen without delay. They were well aware of their limited shop space and took little persuading to join him in taking the vacant shop next to his own. His proposal was to link the two shops by removing a section of the common wall, but create two separate shop windows. The concept was totally new. In London and elsewhere there were boutiques but no 'His and Hers'. The trio, prior to their bonanza with boys, had run a pub and rejected his Op Art decor in favour of a retro theme: a large Victorian bar. A horseshoe-shaped bar was built to link the two shops together and the interior furnished to faithfully reflect the period. A large brewery and pub chain supplied items free, simply to give themselves more warehouse space. They were of course busy embracing recessed fluorescent lighting, polystyrene ceiling tiles, plastic laminates with chrome, and washable vinyl seating throughout their pubs.

The shop made a big impact and the takings were initially spectacular. His new partners had natural flair for retail selling, enhanced by their recent success. The idea was to offer something to the young beyond just clothing, so records, cosmetics, and Coca-Cola were stocked. Customers could drink a Coke at the bar as they listened to the latest pop music. The era for popular listening was unrivaled before or since: Motown, Beatles, Stones, soul and blues seemed to arrive all at once, from nowhere. Pop music, as with fashion, had never been so loud, new and daring. In fashion, tights were new. Without them, mini- and then micro-skirts were unthinkable. Colours too were worn together successfully that hitherto were thought in the worst taste. All in all, things augured well for the shop. As an added attraction a live band occasionally played for the Saturday trade. The shop was called Coke and Clobber, with a trading motif in red and gold: a sun with a smiling face.

But the sun frowned on the girls' department. New glamour notwithstanding, girls did not have the spending power. And the natural inclination of their sex to dress had always been catered for in a mass-market at low prices. So the girls' side did not do its figures and the new investors became disgruntled. The girls were dragging them down and they began to feel they had been duped.

There were other problems. Two of the three new business partners were a couple who came to run the new shop, leaving their friend at the other. Now, without his colleagues to cramp his style, the business thrived more than ever before under the management of this flamboyant character of 50-odd with a blonde toupée, a specialist at putting gauche youth at ease. These were also the days before electronic stock control: shoplifting could too easily be made the scapegoat for losses when the theft could be internal. Such a prospect began to play upon the couple's collective mind, and all the more because their friend gambled every night.

Perhaps these fears stimulated the pair to compensate themselves for real or imagined losses. As a result they proceeded to buy a stream of nearly-new luxury cars on hire-purchase. Mercedes followed Jaguars in succession. Where did they find the money? Their new and startled partner did not feel he could question them – they were, after all, entitled to continuing profits from their other shop. As to his own role in the new enterprise, he readily conceded the shop's floor to their proven expertise and retreated to the secluded rear to make clothes. These were the sixties, and designers paid no heed to Paris (which never reclaimed its predominant influence). The forum for acceptance or not was the street. The power of fashion is such that even the garish can be acceptable.

The younger of the couple had a flair for publicity, and many fashion shows were run together in another new phenomenon: big discotheques. The newly liberated thronged to these, gyrating to deafening music with pulsating rhythms undreamt of hitherto (jive was never a mass event, though vigorous. Earlier dance and popular song was languorous and romantic.) These were the centenary years of the American Civil War and a customer requested that he make a copy of the suit worn by the Federalist general, Ulysses S. Grant. The garment was restrained in style yet imposing, so he made a further suit and took it to London where he obtained an order for a dozen. Unlike his partners, his means of transport were modest. To promote the shop he bought a second-hand van and painted it in the shop's red, white, and gold livery. It was bought from a butcher on a frosty day and he thought the price reasonable, but as the weather warmed it began to smell of rotten meat. Nothing, it seemed, could be done to get rid of the odour. When he delivered the clothes to London's Carnaby Street, 'Lord John' hastened out, keen to collect his order. Opening the van doors he was knocked backwards by the stench, but accepted the suits – such is the power of fashion! A connection facilitated an order for several dozen from Orbachs in New York. They were all returned, citing poor manufacture. He had given the work to a tailor familiar only with ladies' tailoring. The ensuing dispute with the tailor responsible dragged on for years.

Something, he felt, could be done with the shop's Coca-Cola bottle tops. Drilling four holes in the edge of each, he linked them together and after lining the chain-mail effect, created a girl's bikini (Paco Rabanne in Paris much later achieved success with his medallioned clothes.) The city's paper ran a photograph of a model in the swimsuit. Encouraged, he took the bikini to Coca-Cola's London office, where he was ushered into a middle-manager's office, feeling confident in the potential of his creation when worn by a pretty girl. The reception he received rendered him incapable of reply. The man said, "The thing is only of interest because they're our bottle tops." This fact was so obvious that the visitor expected the man to continue and to admit the bikini's potential. Instead, the remark was intended to close the interview. Dumbfounded, he staggered from the building. He lacked the experience, or whatever, to realise that he should have approached a more senior executive and not just a dedicated young jobsworth.

He continued making efforts to drum up business, hiring a well-known local pop group to play at the shop. The idea, novel for the time, attracted much interest not least because the music was deafening. These were times before council byelaws banned excessive noise. Generally, the strictures of old conformities shrank from confrontation with what was glaringly new and exciting. The day went well and attracted the Saturday shopping crowd into the street. One could say that with the council's desertification 'planning process', this was what it took.

Late that night he received a call from the police. The shop was on fire. Arrived at the scene together with the fire-engine was a jeering mob turned out from the pub at closing time. Having experienced the dishonesty of some of the population he was disappointed that these people should suspect and disapprove so vocally of a similar imagined capacity in others. The fire was extinguished, the premises were secured and he returned home to bed. Asleep once more, he was woken again by the police: the fire had restarted. Re-attending a fire that in their professional competence they considered dealt with did not please the firemen and they were suspicious. However, on examination it was accepted that the fire was not deliberate and had probably been caused by an overloaded circuit caused by the pop group's equipment that day.

The insurance company, as required by independent loss-adjusters, met its obligations and provided an opportunity for his partners to buy themselves a new car. But the shop, though restocked, still fell short of its break-even target. If completely new stock couldn't turn the ship around, what could? Increasingly there was an atmosphere of gloom. It did not help matters that his partners were unable to say he had duped them into joining him: it had been their own decision and he too suffered the same loss.

With the situation as it stood, both evident and impenetrable, he decided to look for premises on his own account in London. New ventures beckon the gullible with optimism, and in forgoing his salary too, through his absence, the shop would benefit. Having endured the consequences of Bristol Council planning, his watchword was now pedestrian flow. Traversing every populous shopping district on foot, he found teeming hordes – the retailers' dream – which gave him much encouragement. So with his father's remaining gift of capital he sought an old property to lease and renovate to his advantage. He chose at last a run-down shop in a street market said to be the oldest in England. Six days a week a throng surged among stalls jammed wheel to wheel. The stalls obscured the shopfronts but in the pavement's gap behind, a crowd too pushed by. The stalls' customers, he noted, unlike some of their owners, were poor. Many had been moved and re-housed from blitzed docklands in the East End. The fruit and vegetables on offer were the rejected produce from other markets but the ever-hopeful innocent was impressed by their number and in any case he aimed to give them something they could afford.

A designer and manufacturing friend had offered him the very advantageous terms of sale-or-return if he were to open a shop in London. Her clothes had sold reasonably well in Bristol and were hampered only in that market by price and sophistication. They were 'trendy' – that new term – and often mini-skirted and figure-hugging in open-weave crocheted jersey. He could hardly wait to put the whole concept to the test.

As to the economic flavour of the area and the times, this huge London borough had been but lightly touched by the Macmillan Tories' 'you've-never-had-it-so-good' era. The young still living at home had new spending power, but their elders struggled. There had now been four years of Socialist government, and inflation stimulated by constant strikes had ushered in a new form of austerity christened 'stagflation'. Interest on savings and investment was well below the rate of inflation but people (unless young and carefree) were obliged to keep their money close despite this, to deal with constant price rises. The magic of a floating exchange rate to re-ignite activity was still some years distant.

Social changes from the recent past were a happy 'bread-and-circuses' sop to the feckless ('only the really poor may be truly profligate') so off-course betting was now permitted, and betting shops well attended by men at any time of day sprang up everywhere and many of their womenfolk wagered their housekeeping money in the vast new bingo halls. The government was careful not to tax alcohol beyond people's reach, and breweries responded to this policy by creating new bars distinct from traditional pubs. Garish and carpeted, they were intended to offer an environment of new respectability where a young man might bring his fancy. Hitherto, girls had generally avoided pubs for outings even if escorted.

The rear of one of these new enterprises was opposite our protagonist's premises. Bars on each of its five floors occupied the entire building of a redundant newspaper. After the street market closed each evening the newcomers became the sole street occupants. He was 30 and his friend to assist in the renovation was 18. By night the narrow street was unlit, and given this new phenomenon almost cynically targeted at youths, unruly behaviour was a nightly occurrence. Peering anxiously out at the scene below, the pair soon realised that their requests for police intervention would go unheeded. One victim slowly buckled at the knees, sinking to the ground only after repeated beatings to the head with a light fruit crate. Others rushed at each other with market hand-carts or threw crates from an overhead walkway onto those below.

More remarkable were the events that the occupants of his newly leased premises may have witnessed some 15 years earlier. What took place within full view from the building had a greater influence on the eventual abolition of capital punishment in Britain than any other incident. Escaping along the roof of a Customs tobacco bonded warehouse, two burglars were challenged by police. One of them was below the age of full criminal responsibility and, responding to his older accomplice's call to "Let him have it, Chris!", shot the policeman dead. Despite much public outcry the older man was hanged. Fifty years on and a new twist is added: it has now been reported that Christopher Craig now states that Derick Bentley did not call out to him at all.

The dilapidated building of three floors and a deep basement had at least a watertight roof, a lavatory and washbasin. One of a row in a jerrybuilt mid-Victorian terraces, it had unceremoniously and contrary to its design become an 'end of terrace': its supporting neighbour had simply been shorn off and a supermarket built where it once stood. Fortunately, the end wall (hitherto just a dividing wall) seemed safe enough. It leaned inwards, as is usual, drawn in by the weight of the floors which are safely pinched tight in turn. Evident though this was to anyone, the new tenant obtained a full structural survey for peace of mind. Beyond advising that a steel beam placed to support the first floor was overstressed and approaching its critical bending moment, and therefore might collapse, the surveyor reported nothing untoward.

The keen young men soon had the dubious beam supported by a round steel pillar passing through the entrance floor and grounded in the basement. They then set about more important matters, making quaint changing cubicles for the 'dolly birds' who were expected to grace the premises. After some days they noticed that the man with the market stall obscuring the front of the shop spent most of his time watching them. His stall, meagrely set out with sweets in jars, attracted few customers. A discreet inquiry revealed that in fact he owned the building, which thanks to his wife had once been a successful sweet shop. Unable to continue following her death, he had closed and leased out the shop. His new tenant was unaware of this, having dealt only with the agents.

It did not take long to realise why the sweets had been kept in jars. The building ran with mice. Each evening as the market fell quiet they sallied forth from their runs inside the walls. As these were of brick and soft lime mortar, generations of mice had tunnelled everywhere. To share one's living space with vermin is not just demeaning but debilitating. After a hard day putting the building to rights the pair's spirits sank as those mice not actually visible could be heard screeching as they mated and fought. The mouse, like the hare, is a prairie animal and its nature is to roam, whereas the rat and rabbit stay close to their nest or warren. Little could be done to eradicate them. Filling gaps was insufficient because the sagging floors left the skirting boards attached to the walls so the mice ran in and out through the resulting gap. In their immediate concern for themselves it did not cross the workers' minds how girls in changing rooms would react to mice.

The pair soldiered on while the owner outside gaped, distracted and unheeding of requests for his stall's fruit gums. He would stand in puddles of rain rather than pass up the opportunity to watch the foolish *goy* soak his building with money and labour. Furthermore, the *goy* was confused. From whence he hailed (the new dominions) Jewish people were synonymous with success. A 'poor Jew' as a concept would be oxymoronic. The 'threadbare Jewish tailor' escaped from the pogroms of Eastern Europe to the East End of London was as implausible to this newcomer as the dottiest art film. Jews were synonymous with success, and if they tripped they were soon on their feet again.

Yet his landlord, a nice mild man, was not poor, as he owned the building. Therefore, standing in the rain, he was content to join in this caricature in folklore of 'the poor East End Jew'. The newcomers slowly became aware of the unique culture of the street. It was the sixties and a period now assessed as remarkable for the power and influence held by a handful of London criminal families. Street markets were awash with unattributable cash so of course the families were present. There were boxing families too. A pub licensee had bravely but unsuccessfully fought the world heavyweight champion. It was all strange to the new boy. In his uncomplicated country, control, threat and violence were the random acts of individuals, not clans.

In the sixties, income-taxation control of cash business, from street stalls to the most expensive antique shop, was lax, inasmuch as a dealer's own assessment of his income tended to be accepted. At a time when air travel was expensive one stall holder had been taking holidays in California for years. The time was still distant when tax inspectors said, "We know you're taking £X so don't tell us you're taking

£Y." However, to be safe from the taxman such dealers could not safely maintain a large bank balance, so they were obliged to stash their cash at home – with the attendant risks. The stallholder landlord, aged about 60, seemed to think he had done well in being 'worked over' just three times. In being robbed, he implied, he would be safe from similar attention from rival gangs, and in that manner would be protected.

It was obvious that with the shopfront obscured by the landlord's stall, a window placed in the shop's end wall would be an advantage. It would make the premises more visible and offer a clear view of the street. Examining the problem, the pair discovered with horror that the three-storey unrendered brick-and-old-lime-mortar wall was just four inches thick, and not, as the surveyor had stated, of nine-inch-thick double brick. With delivery lorries to the neighbouring supermarket rumbling by at the wall's foot (to say nothing of swarms of passers-by) the situation was frightening. The negligence of the surveyor was plainly actionable, as it was on his advice that the tenant had accepted the lease. A remedy in court could extend to the surveyor being liable in damages for the rent. Such an action would necessitate interruption of all work and the anxieties that attend – 'the law's delays'. So he swallowed hard and faced the problem. Somehow, they would have to make the wall safe and then insert the window.

Scaffolding could not be erected, as it would block the supermarket's deliveries. The only alternative, a ladder, was worrying as the lane was steep so the ladder's foot had to be chocked. No insurance company would grant cover – which at least made clear that the wall needed attention! The lime mortar was crumbling and brought to mind stories of the Blitz, where such walls had so little strength that bomb blasts blew bricks down in showers like confetti. Wobbling each in turn on the ladder, applying a strong cement render, they were at least grateful that the building's weight pulled the wall inwards and away from them.

Experience of the omnipotence of councils cautioned him to inquire as to whether he could set a window in the wall. After deliberation the council considered they had assumed ownership when the rest of the terrace had been demolished. He knew better than to ask why 'their' wall was in a life-threatening condition and they did not protest when they imposed a 'license fee' for their consent. Mentioning the need to lay a new drain, he inquired about the location of the sewer, to be told that they had no idea, and would he kindly let them know when he found it? The lofty oak-paneled council chambers were impressive indeed, as befitted these worthies, who simply had no idea of the whereabouts of their sewers. It was well that these events enjoyed an aspect of novelty. Working together on varied and unusual tasks, the pair, too, were great friends. The younger was committed by inclination to skilled manual tasks requiring imagination; the elder found the hard work an opiate, however temporary, to his intractable problems in Bristol.

So down and down they dug in their quest for the sewer. It was not just a matter of strong backs dictating to weak minds: they wanted to succeed! The engineer consulted for the window construction, to their great pleasure, considered them capable of performing the procedures necessary to break through the wall, take its load and set the steel-framed window in place. 'Needles' – large timber baulks – were passed through the pierced wall after the floor's load was 'picked up' by temporary adjustable acrow-props. Two baulks ('dead shores') were then placed outside the building vertically under each of the two needles. Then under each were placed two opposing and interlocking 'folding wedges' and in precise rhythm together they were tapped up tight by the two with sledgehammers on either side in order to take the building's load above the aperture. The gap opened, the frame was set in place and grouted into the surrounding brickwork with concrete the consistency of brown sugar. After a few days the dead shores were 'struck' (removed) to complete the work.

Such pleasurable distraction ended abruptly when he examined his bank balance. He did not have sufficient funds to both pay the rent and finish fitting out the shop. A bank? No: he held property only in partnership. An advance from his supplier? He knew she did not have such resources and anyway was offering her dresses on sale-or-return at a considerable burden. So he was left with an improved building and any prospects for it quite out of his hands. But it was enhanced with improvements and he was sanguine about his chances of re-leasing it at a small profit. The landlord outside, too, still gaped in admiration.

Some weeks passed and agents had not received one inquiry. The situation resembled his predicament in Bristol: in neither place could the leases be assigned, as no one wanted the premises. Yet in both places the lessees remained liable for the rent. He was getting close to defaulting: the intensity of the Labour government's credit squeeze defied belief. Few people would venture their savings in a new business enterprise. Despite the commercial gloom there was unprecedented gaiety in the street. Transistor radios had become cheap only recently and stalls were well stocked. Naturally, these blared forth the hits of the moment. One song in particular was iconic for the mood of the time. It was played through the summer and beyond: "If you're going to San Francisco / Be sure to wear some flowers in your hair ..."

Flowers aptly set the mood and scene. Unusually for the sixties, the summer was long and warm. The young had wrested leadership in fashion and had been defying convention since the start of the decade. In 1967 it was as if the zany mocking of life had been embraced too well by the population at large. The Beatles had enjoyed years of ascendancy and were now so well embraced by the Establishment they stood for it themselves. Youth knows when things cloy. For them a year is compressed to a month and their elders can never catch up. Youth was soon in the vanguard again: 'flower power' blew over from the United States.

This languid and laconic movement left an indelible impression. The message, 'Relax, do your own thing', was unsettling. Unconsciously, he still sought protection in old conventions. But now young males wore kaftans with coloured braids in their hair.

His situation drove him to seek advice from a stall holder. And this with some effort. It was not that he was stand-offish, but simply that he lacked the guile to enter their world. An insincere attempt to do so would be obvious. On asking what he could do with the building, the answer came: "The street needs a chipper." He soon saw his funds did not run to equipping one. Even with hire-purchase he lacked the deposit for a fryer. Then, to his amazement, a salesman offered to accept his first few weeks takings in lieu. So, from that blessed life-saving moment he and his pal were in the fish-and-chip business.

Of course things had to be re-arranged. The seductive Turkish changing rooms were swiftly dismantled and taken in the former meat van back to Bristol. Then they cut fish shapes out in tiles to their own design over the shop's walls. The helpful salesman advised that a fish supplier offered a three-day fish-and-chip-frying course at no charge in the distant northeast, so off they went. They learnt that central to successful functioning was the temperature of the pans. Too hot and the business could catch fire, and even if it did not, customers might not wait until the oil cooled down. Too cold, and again they could disappear. Anticipation and preparation in advance for the expected race was essential. Feverish 'catch-up' operations leaving the pans unattended could see them catch fire or, because of that fear, go cold – were to be avoided. Plainly, two operators were essential.

They were not so insensitive as not to notice raised eyebrows in the street: did they know what they were doing? Fish and chips to Londoners are a staple like mother's milk and must be 'just so'. As opening day drew nigh they did indeed grow fearful, and to his lasting shame, on returning from Bristol he lost his nerve and poached a girl serving at a fish-and-chip shop in a neighbouring suburb. For more money she agreed to start when they opened in two weeks. There was still much to do: a serving counter in particular. Things were looking up; they would seize the carrot of success before the stick could beat them.

Of course he was taking too much for granted. Optimism won't race without the chance of a fall. His friend had endured weeks of promises that he would be paid up to date as soon as cash was in the till. But now he put his foot down and demanded immediate payment if he was to continue. Somehow our protagonist found the money (and echoes say, "Isn't that always the way?"). Then cash and pal rushed up the road together. With regret, and now alone, the elder saw his fault. He had not kept his pal 'square'.

The shop's supplies of fish and potatoes were due in days as he struggled to build the counter, something his friend was decidedly better at doing. Thankfully the new laminates and glues covered the gaps in the joinery beneath. There was plenty to do. He lacked the time and imagination to reflect that the stallholders standing outside in all weathers put great store in a 'chippy' opening at last in their midst. But there was time to recall a remark his father had made to him only half in jest: "You couldn't run a fish-and-chip shop: if you didn't forget the fish you'd forget the chips." So he checked the list of necessaries – a grim task as all non-comestibles were on hire-purchase. He would have to sustain himself on any fish and chips he couldn't sell.

He 'lit the pans', got the temperature up, and opened the doors to business. First through the door a very polite man in working clothes presented himself. He had heard the shop was opening and advised the novice should not continue without help, and putting it delicately, offered his services for the busy times when chaos might reign and money might not be made. After accepting the gentleman's services, the listener soon saw the point: the trade came in intense bursts, mostly at lunchtime, when people could not wait or were not prepared to.

This expert already had two jobs, and as is not unusual even among otherwise astute people with a financial responsibility, went out to work to keep a shop. This was a greengrocery in a poor, respectable but hard-up suburb of privately-owned houses. Eddie, in his late fifties, related how a neighbour parked his lorry some way off and changed out of overalls into a business suit before walking with his briefcase to his house. Eddie's wife ran the shop while he was head fryer in a big fish restaurant on the high street. He combined this with a job as cellarman in a pub which was handily placed near to his third employer. He had a perfect amiable style with customers while his awkward employer could not establish any rapport at all with the salt of the earth: hidebound in his antipodean, egalitarian view, he saw no need to try.

This brilliant operator obviously worked short hours, given his commitments. His introverted pupil took refuge through operating a wall range. In so doing he had his back to the customer, could prepare the order, spin round, and say, "Two and tuppence please." Inevitably there was some pressure from the street. A regular potato supply was a problem for the whole country: it was feast or famine. Unsurprisingly, stall holders offered to supply. British-grown potatoes were often poor: soft and dark through forcing with nitrogen. Small operators would rent a field as a speculation. Sometimes the country had to rely on supplies from the Mediterranean, whose potatoes were often small and the bags full of dirt and stones to increase the weight. One or two stallholders, marched in unbidden, dumped bags in a cloud of dust, and announced, "Here are your potatoes." He had to be firm and refuse them. It was a welcome relief to see Eddie's smiling face on his visits. As ladies with pushchairs and their children conversed at length, dropping paper from sixpenn'orth chips and squashing not a few underfoot, Eddie was quite relaxed. A natural gentleman, he was ever tolerant in his environment: 'as happy as a pig in muck'. It seems this metaphor was not inappropriate, as he related an incident from his past: when war came Eddie got a government contract removing nightsoil from army camps. This was a 'reserved occupation' so he was not liable for war service. Following the evacuation from Dunkirk the Channel coast teemed with thousands of soldiers preparing to resist invasion, so Eddy's resources were somewhat stretched. Venturing into their fields, many farmers found they had had an unwelcome delivery.

Eddie was the only ray of sunshine in a perpetual nightmare. Laden with hire-purchase debt on frying range, peeling, chipping and tea machines, chicken and pie cookers and refrigerator, plus overheads, the proprietor had to keep open for all the hours God made. Retaining a woman to rely upon by day was difficult; late into the night, impossible. Running a fish-and-chip shop alone with a waiting queue could be likened to a one-legged man's attempts to walk a tightrope. Apart from twice-weekly drunken mayhem, the street was often deserted.

Yet lit like a lighthouse, the chipper attracted some late-night revelers from the distant high street. Mercifully, this was still a time when people (especially youth) were more restrained in their behaviour. They were not yet, drunk or sober, sweeping through towns in phalanxes of 12 or so forcing others into the roadway. So he did not so much fear for his person, only felt exposed to embarrassment and silent ridicule.

Erring on caution to avoid a pan fire, and also economising on heat in case trade was lacking, made him vulnerable to the consequences of long delays if suddenly a queue should develop. Nothing drops a pan's temperature like a bucket of newly-chipped potatoes. With a long wait on their hands, it was the women rather than their escorts who would follow him out to the preparation room and make free with comments. With women, if he could secure their help, he avoided all adventure, fearing compromise. On the one occasion when through sheer misery he did succumb, the consequences were as might be expected: placed in charge of the till, she ran off with it. Desperate again for help just for a day or two he telephoned his girlfriend in Bristol, but she declared that she "had not been educated by a governess to work in a fish-and-chip shop".

But there was a ray of hope. He could show that despite his overheads he was trading at a profit. Through the trade magazine he put the business on the market. Almost immediately an agent replied that he was holding a deposit for an interested client. Weeks of anxious waiting passed and his own young solicitor seemed to accept and agree that the agent held the deposit instead of the solicitor himself. Eventually, he learned that the agent made similar assurances to anyone advertising their business for sale. Misery reigned once more.

In the shop, despite his attention to cleanliness, frying odours excited the mice. The door clanging shut at closing time was their signal to appear. With adhesive and rubber coving round the walls he kept them out of the shop itself, but upstairs he shared his living space with them. He soon found that these vermin were the ideal accompaniment to more bad news. His accountant rang from Bristol. His partners had abandoned the business, leaving just a young assistant in their place. He sat slumped in the kitchen, overwhelmed by his dilemma. He could not leave one shop to go to the aid of the other. A mouse appeared – hardly alarming – but then another … two means yet more, and that's a plague. He climbed on to the table and, as all humans do at some time in their lives, he bellowed in despair. This helped, if only because the next stage can be more drastic. So he climbed down from the table and up to the attic to bed.

Each morning there was now an added dimension to his routine: phoning Bristol. Had they had a better day? No. Almost always no. His accountant interviewed prospective managers. He himself could not attend. The applicants were not promising. Demographically, the baby-boomers, the population increase following the war, had not yet reached the labour market. Later it was said of the time that a chimpanzee could have got a job – such was the labour shortage.

So there was much to contemplate as he cut the rock salmon (the dogfish preferred by Londoners) into lozenge shapes to make it look bigger. The smell of ammonia peculiar to these sharks never ceased to amaze him. Then there were the little red worms often wriggling in cod fillets – thoroughly alive even if the fish had been frozen. Then Eddie dropped by: "You'd better be careful, you could get a slap." Unfamiliar with Londoners' capacity for understatement, he thought this meant a mild rebuke. Eventually he realised the euphemism: 'slap' ran the whole gamut up to grievous bodily harm. He was confident he had not caused offence in the market but took note to improve his demeanour.

Then it was Eddie's turn to worry. The police were giving him trouble. In his part-time job as cellarman a case of whisky had gone missing and the police kept calling at his house, determined to obtain a confession. Eddie was an honest man, and the persistent accusations brought him very low, with the result that he could help out no longer. For the proprietor now there was one ironic comfort: the situation in Bristol was even worse than that in which he stood. Surely, he thought, one fine day someone would see the extra potential in an already profitable business. Meanwhile, he continued to open six days a week, all day until midnight, as weeks strained by without an inquiry.

On Sundays a new friend called by car with his young family and took him to the sea. The kind man had seen his predicament and with this gesture no doubt preserved his sanity. Alex, a Hungarian, had escaped from the violent revolution of 1956. Perhaps because he was homesick for his country, his marriage to an English girl was unhappy. For a living he built fitted wardrobes into bedrooms. Tall, blond and handsome, he said gloomily, "I always tell them I'm married."

At last a buyer appeared. The Greek Cypriot was not impressed with the operation and plainly thought that three or four times the profit should be obtained from each portion, which in turn should be half the size. Customers, he said, must be invited to consider one by one the merits of individual pieces of fish displayed in lighted cabinets. Astounded, the desperate vendor, given his knowledge of the stallholders' expectations, thought the prospective purchaser either magician or madman. So he forgot him, but then shortly the deposit was paid, then contracts exchanged with acceptance of all hire-purchase liabilities agreed. The day of settlement arrived and the gentleman announced he would not accept some of the equipment. The temptation to capitulate was overwhelming, but somehow our protagonist clung on and declined to complete. The man left him in despair, but he was soon distracted by a regular who had come to expect as of right a piece of middle skate three inches thick. The Cypriot, coming as he did from the Mediterranean (to do him kindness) knew only an occasional glut of sardines, whereas Britain was still an island of coal surrounded by fish. Soon the fish stocks were depleted and the coal discredited; oil, God's last gift to England, was still some years away

The desperate situation in Bristol somehow put matters in a different light. It was sufficient relief on any given day to hear that the shop had taken enough money to pay the bailiffs who were calling the next. And if there was not, grim warnings from these gentlemen distracted him from problems which in perspective were relatively minor. The fish-and-chip treadmill continued, and as he had not given in to the Cypriot he could only hope for another buyer. Then one day his solicitor phoned to say the man had accepted the original terms.

He and his girlfriend now pooled all their resources to buy a half-share in a dilapidated house for conversion to flats. They had bought one similar prior to his London adventure. Without doubt had he not done so the money would have gone into the business. Few experiences in life are more demoralising than waiting for customers to enter one's shop. Paint dries and grass grows faster than people will come through the door. The dreaded consequences of failing to 'do the figures' seeps into the bones. The slow march to the scaffold begins with insistence on payment in advance. Fewer and fewer manufacturers will grant normal 30-day credit terms. Therefore the chance for the retailer to make a profit on the delivery before he must pay for it is removed. Next, the range of merchandise diminishes as the number of suppliers is reduced. This is the moment for a manufacturer to do well. If he holds his nerve he can become almost the sole supplier, and as the business struggles on choose his moment (usually with few bills outstanding) to 'pull the plug' and abruptly cease deliveries.

During these proceedings, other predatory fish attend the feast. Hoping, as with the last supplier, that the death agony will be long and profitable, they are civil, even jolly as they visit their patient each Monday with a cheery "Be sure to have another good Saturday!" And in this these bailiffs are often lucky. The 'must-have' fever of teenagers for a craze can fill a till, which is as well as the sheriffs to the City Corporation added 17.5 percent to the writ after court costs for scant trouble.

In the late sixties there was an entirely new phenomenon: a poster craze. This ran for about a year until everyone had as many as they could fit on their walls and it abruptly ended. New printing techniques had made possible a display of any subject matter – simply decorative or as cartoons. They fitted well with the other stock – records, cosmetics, Coca-Cola and popular fashion. In harmony with the new relaxed sexual behaviour of the time, one cartoon depicted a girl fully clothed, seated on top of a step ladder with her legs apart. She wore too, a big smile, fishnet stockings and a Texan ten-gallon hat. At the bottom of the ladder stood a tiny man, formally dressed in an overcoat and homburg. As if taken by surprise the man was peering sheepishly over his shoulder. The caption read: "What's a nice guy like you doing in a place like this?"

The caption was small, so he took a lipstick from stock, rewrote it in bold, beautiful red, and placed the poster in the shop window. On the same day he received a visit from a plain-clothes policeman. Following a complaint from a member of the public the police were seeking advice on the matter from the Crown Prosecution Service in London. A female traffic warden had been offended by the poster.

He was appalled. What were these people talking about? Bought from a London printer, the posters were on sale all over Britain. Soon he was told prosecution would follow under the Indecent Advertisements Act 1899. It was no trouble – even a pleasure – to provide evidence for magistrates to show that the case was an absurdity. The Bristol City Corporation was promoting and funding an Arts Centre performance with a brochure depicting nudity and sex on its cover. In London the notorious theatrical revue 'Oh! Calcutta' had been running for years. The *Sunday Times* had more recently displayed the brothel paintings of Toulouse-Lautrec. Soon he learned he had been charged, and a court hearing set. On the appointed day he found arrayed on the bench ladies bearing a startling resemblance to the three he had encountered in his unsuccessful rating appeal three years earlier. They wore similar hats, piled up and floral, one a large orb of imitation pink cyclamen. As with royalty on civic duty, their hats were unbrimmed so the wearers could be seen. Confidently, the accused put his 'open-and-shut case' to this triumvirate. Were they uniformly perplexed, stolid or just vacant as they listened, he wondered? Bringing to their notice the printed material in his support he concluded his evidence.

"Do you plead guilty or not guilty?" their chairman asked. At that instant he was kneeling before the Mother Superior as she struck him repeatedly with her belt. To avoid more punishment, although innocent and uncomprehending, he must plead guilty. On coming to the country had his father too not told him he was riddled with guilt? So guilty it must be and "Guilty" he replied.

The ladies hesitated. Plainly, following a convincing defence they expected a 'not guilty' plea to dismiss the case. They could not know that, put before authority to answer any charge at all, his instinct was to plead guilty. They retired for some minutes and on returning the view prevailed that he had pleaded guilty therefore he must be guilty. He was fined £10 with £10 costs.

Matters remained as pressing as ever at the shop. Had the intent of their visits not been so serious the bailiffs would have made a perfect comedy act resembling Ronnie Corbett and Ronnie Barker. Perfect troupers turning up each week, they never missed a performance. Closing the business with the protection of limited-liability company status was not an option, as he was liable for the lease. No-one in their senses would assume the lease of premises in such a poor location, even though with inflation the rent in real terms was falling. The greatest burden on the business was the rates, unfailingly increased each year beyond the rate of inflation. Decidedly, corporations of the people are without conscience. Adjoining units too remained unlet, and who had left him to assume the lease alone? There were now three of them, as before, in the original shop that had proved such a gold mine. Now the monopoly on trends in fashion they once enjoyed had ended with new competitors, so the returning couple persuaded a brewery to open a nightclub. The more persuasive of the two sat on a throne awaiting customers. Few came, and the brewery lost its money. The third remained in the shop, his gambling continued and he was bankrupted. A particular grievance was that the receiver even took his dead mother's wedding ring.

He learnt that a shop was doing exceptional business in Cardiff. It might be tempting, he thought, for the owner to have a branch in another city not too far distant. Arrived at the premises, he was encouraged to see that they were very small; the owner might well like a larger shop and, moreover, one that had had a considerable turnover. Confidently, he suggested that the man join him and offered the owner, at no cost, half of the business. The reply was: "What's half of nothing?" It took some days before he grasped the meaning of the man's remark. In this, someone who had made their own money would have had less difficulty.

His background in life had led him to assume almost everyone was honest. So he rejected a more worldly friend's suggestion of checking any possibility of theft by his own manager. As trade was so bad, the simple method outlined by his friend posed no problems. Someone unknown to the manager was to enter the shop at a specified time and purchase an expensive suit. At the end of the day's trading, the sales records and the cash should be in the till. If the number of suits on offer was known at the outset, the exercise was foolproof. Regrettably, our protagonist did not follow this course of action. Not to trust a manager he had appointed himself, combined with a latent belief in the honesty of his fellow man, deterred him; furthermore, put simply, he had not made his own money. Further consequences of his lack of vigilance followed. As it is essential in fashion retailing to see what the competition have in their windows, the manager made a brisk daily tour just after opening. Much later – too much later – he heard that this trip also involved a visit to the betting shop.

At about this time he received a letter from his father in America: would he join him on a camper-van trip? It was obvious he would do the driving while his father and girlfriend remained in the capacious rear. Nonetheless the offer was tempting, especially in those distant days when such travel was new and the roads uncrowded. Some years earlier his father had invited him to join a yacht he had chartered in the Caribbean. The son, as with this kind offer, declined as his business situation was even more desperate than described. These invitations for holidays seemed in contradiction to his father's strictures of dedication to work at all times. Undeterred, his father wrote again, but not a third time. Not much later his girlfriend related that he did not want to suffer a further refusal.

His father died suddenly in Florida. He met his father's consort at the airport. Distressed, she told him of the grim and cruel event. It appeared that the mercenary American medical system then pervading was the cause. Heavy smoking and resulting emphysema required the father to take oxygen, especially at night. Cylinders were bought from the local grocer and mistakes or confusion as to the method of payment arose. Perhaps cash before rather than on delivery was expected. At the appointed time the oxygen was not delivered, leading to a frightening death. The heat and humidity of Florida did not help his condition. As they drove, the lady recalled how the smell of new-mown hay had reminded the father of how hard he had to work as a young immigrant farmhand in New Zealand.

Some weeks elapsed. At his father's accountant's request he had readily consented to meet the fiancée (as she may well have been) on her arrival, and for some time heard no more. A letter then followed asking him to collect his father's effects, clothing, and papers on their arrival from the US, and forward them to the accountant, who was one of two executors. Complying, the son reflected that he had met the man but once and that he was memorable (often though that is judged unkindly) for his fixed smile.

Months passed, and he heard nothing more. Insofar as he vaguely considered there might be a will, he did not entertain expectations. He was almost at the bottom of the money so generously given. This too had been passed against his father's opinion that people were ever the better for making their own way. The father's ex-wife had prevailed, and he had made this gift to please her. For the moment his days were filled with attempts to obtain credit in advance for clothes to sell. The comedy act of the bailiffs would continue for only as long as they could be satisfied and give their parting cheery wave, saying again, "Be sure you have a good Saturday!" With the shop providing little income, out of shop hours he spent as much time as possible converting the two houses and seeking tenants.

Finally, with one supplier increasingly able to dictate terms, the death throes of a retail operation resemble that of any living thing. Optimism (remission), and pessimism (relapse) alternate. The owner is both patient and doctor, and will keep himself (his creation) alive at all costs. An occasional day of good sales mitigates the bad.

With assistance at last refused by his local bank there remained only as a last resort his bank in London. Clutching at a straw, he hoped that though they had seen his account run down steadily of late, there might be some goodwill since he had earlier held a large untouched balance for a long period. Embarrassment, even shame, may have caused him to arrive unprepared. He had not sought advice from, for example, his accountant (though, to be generous, these were the days before people spoke easily of 'business plans'.) He simply wanted an overdraft; didn't lots of people have one?

A counter cashier was hardly the man to whom one should address such a request, and he soon returned with a nonchalant refusal. Faced suddenly with stark reality, the consequences that must follow were convincing. Making an effort to leave with dignity, he allowed himself the luxury of feeling a little aggrieved. This headquarters of the Royal Bank of Canada had earlier 'lost' his paid-in cheque for the entire proceeds from the sale of the fish-and-chip business. Despite being told that he held a franked paying-in stub, they refused for some weeks to admit receipt, and even after the cheque finally cleared they still refused to offer any explanation or apology. In times before he was given money, the same bank had hounded him continually over a negative balance of £50. Decidedly, he thought, his approach had ever been too timorous.

Before leaving, he withdrew his meager balance and closed the account, but forgot to wipe his feet as a gesture of contempt before stepping from the bank's marbled halls. The shame was all the more intense as he had not made the money himself. There is always that feeling that it's not yours to lose

Unfamiliar with the city, he looked at his map to retrace his steps and return to Bristol. He saw that Lothbury, where he stood, was near Old Broad Street, the address of his father's accountant, Mr Buckley Sharp. Humiliation being thus far the order of his day, he felt he was hardly risking much more were he to pay the gentleman a visit. Sudden appearances without appointments are not in general welcomed, and especially not by those confident of their professional standing. Mr Sharp neither rose to greet him nor offered him a chair. As he had been announced by a secretary, the man knew who his visitor was. Given the general circumstances and his lackey-like compliance hitherto to the executor's requests, at least some polite affability was in order. None was forthcoming, so the supplicant could only state his business: "I wondered whether or not I am mentioned in my father's will?"

"As a matter of fact you are ... I am one of two executors, the other is Miss Joan Rubinstein, the solicitor in the administration. The matter is ... complicated." He did not offer his visitor a copy of the will or suggest that he seek clarification from the solicitors; nor did the visitor press the matter. Only later did he learn that the courts in general grant to an administrator a period of time – the 'executor's year'. Given his personal circumstances he had no family members or experienced friends who could offer advice. Nonetheless, on this day it appeared that his prospects had unexpectedly improved. Pointedly, no further explanation was forthcoming, nor notice as to when he might receive any, so he thanked the man and left.

Many weeks passed. The shop struggled on and he made progress with his partner in the two houses. They married and camped in the back of an old delivery van by way of a honeymoon which they took in Ireland. Returning, he received a letter from the executor inviting him to lunch at his club in St James's. There was, the man explained, a 'conflict of interest' arising from the various dispositions at the testator's death. There was an English will dealing solely with dispensations of English property to a legatee and beneficiaries. Unconnected, with quite different stipulations at variance with the will, was a Lichtenstein Foundation administered from Zurich. His father, in order to comply with Swiss regulations, had Swiss residency and maintained a flat in Lausanne. Finally, as a matter to be resolved, and especially controversial regarding a conflict of interest, were the arrangements that flowed from the earlier sale of the testator's and his surviving partner's business, in which they had held 51% and 49% ownership respectively.

The bewildered listener absorbed but a fraction of the foregoing. Impressed with the splendour of the surroundings, he was flattered and anxious to show that he followed something of the complexities outlined. Yet why should he suspect any ulterior motive? If there were problems with the estate's administration, it was his duty to assist. As he ate his fish, Mr Buckley Sharp disclosed in a circumlocutory manner the first of the three conflicts of interest with which he had to contend.

The first conflict, he said, was that he was acting, and continued to act, for the testator's business partner. As is common, to keep things simple and straight he was accountant to both. On selling the business, for a taxation advantage they had entered into a consultancy agreement to supply advice to the purchaser. The agreement had been cleared as legitimate and provided payments over nine years (dependant on consultancy), of never less than £7,000 and never more than £13,000. Six years of this arrangement were yet to run. The two partners had remained together in business, and using this funding stream they had invented a sail-training machine and formed Caribbean companies to sell it. The machine seemed to be a brilliant invention: a sailing counterpart of the famous Link trainer that simulated flight without the trainee pilot leaving the ground. Share certificates were held by the two partners' respective accounts at their Foundations in Zurich, which were to receive the income. However, no sales of the ingenious but elaborate machine had yet been made.

Such was one 'difficulty': one conflict, one 'hat', as specialists are apt to describe the problem when there is more than one to wear.

The second conflict concerned the English will. The property in England comprised a holiday cottage and furniture in storage. The furniture (although Mr Buckley Sharp pointedly did not mention it) was stored awaiting shipment to the US. As confirmed by his companion, the testator had been actively searching for a house following his decision to emigrate. However, the executor had no intention of stating the deceased had acquired a US domicile of choice. With detailed knowledge of the deceased's affairs, his fellow executor and the Estate Duty Office might easily have taken this view. The 'conflict' arising was that, having sold his house, the testator had lodged the proceeds in his English bank account where it had become mixed with the other balances, in contravention of exchange-control regulations. The executor said that the testator (his client) had held the property as an ex-UK resident despite Revenue rules stating that no property should be owned (or even available) for residence. His view was that, because of the relatively small size of the English estate compared with the Foundation, the house proceeds should be included as part of the estate. This seemed both generous and reasonable, and the son willingly agreed in principle so other beneficiaries – his aunts – could benefit more fully.

The third conflict of interest or 'hat' worn by Mr Buckey Sharp concerned the problem that he continued to act for the deceased's business partner, Mr Bruce Duval.

Meeting the Foundation's officers in Zurich, Mr Buckley Sharp advised them that the Lichtenstein funds standing to the testator's credit were, together with the English estate, subject to inheritance tax. Although adamant that they had no obligations to the British tax authorities, they nonetheless disclosed the value to the executor, as the nominated son and sole beneficiary seemed compliant with the executor's advice. The son nonetheless disagreed that his father had not changed his domicile in emigrating to the United States.

Over lunch at his club the executor depicted the landscape as he saw it, and threw in his strategy for good measure. His gullible guest was eating out of his hand. There was even time for asides on (as he intended it to be understood) the unfortunate sentiments of other clients he had known. These had, following the huge cost and crippling taxation after two world wars, left the country because 'England was finished'. Was he censuring these people for wanting to take their British wealth abroad? Did he say it to justify his decision to repatriate the testator's wealth – wealth that he himself had been instrumental in placing? His guest was too impressed to recall Samuel Johnson's aphorism that 'patriotism is the last refuge of a scoundrel', and was all attentive.

In conclusion the executor delivered his masterstroke, which would at least enable him to employ delaying tactics to the advantage of himself and Duval, the surviving partner, if not entirely insulate him from reproach. Directly he requested that in view of the number of hats he was wearing, would his listener please appoint a solicitor to represent himself separately in negotiations. Deftly he had removed himself from sword's length and placed the principal beneficiary of the English estate and the sole nominee of the Foundation in the hands of another with whom he could contend at will.

The son duly complied, and when he telephoned Sharp the latter replied, "Ah, so you've appointed a Jew!" and continued, "In my experience Gentiles appoint Jews and Jews Gentiles." The man was hard-pressed to conceal his pleasure at his success. He now held all the cards. The precept of 'the executor's year' and his 'duty of care' was largely removed.

The son had appointed the only solicitor he knew, who was his own age, 32, and had impressed him with his efficiency and sympathetic manner. There had been no suggestion that he should find a specialist from a top firm. And incidentally, where was the money coming from to pay an advisor? Why, through the executor! Now equipped with a solicitor he did not need, he also held a begging bowl with which to implore the executor as his supplicant for money to pay the man.

Sharp's next tactic was delay. He would send the son's solicitor a long, elaborate, wide-ranging letter to which he would reply promptly seeking clarification and then for weeks on end receive nothing. The 'problem' so often for the executor was the alleged failure of the Bahamian and Cayman Island companies to reply to his queries. In time, however, it became apparent that the 'problem' was that it was he *himself* who had formed the companies! Finally his solicitor observed that Mr Buckley Sharp was 'writing letters to himself'.

Negotiations began. The executor had avoided his duty to administer the English estate. Statutorily, he had no authority with the Foundation and was only invited to express his opinion on estate duty liability (as he chose to see it) and the Caribbean companies. His purpose now was to achieve financial advantage for himself and Mr Duval, the surviving partner. At current values the consultancy payments over the six years remaining totalled more than £1.5 million. Bemused though he was by the executor's obfuscations, the son was confident of his own assessment that the sail-training machine was not commercial viable: it was a white elephant. Though brilliantly conceived, there was simply no need for it, because people preferred learning to sail on the water. The reason his father had been talked into financing it was that he had a friend who owned a socially smart sailing school and regretted turning away the queue of customers who could not find places in his dinghies. But elsewhere in the country, flooded gravel pits with sailing clubs abounded.

Accordingly, the son requested that advanced settlement of the consultancy payment should be negotiated and the proceeds distributed 51 percent and 49 percent between the respective parties. The opposition countered by insisting that the machine was viable: it had been on television, attracted interest at the National Boat Show, and although the simulator was, owing to its complexity, very expensive to buy outright, it could be leased.

The son knew that his father's involvement (and probably his interest) in the project had ended largely with the completion of the machine. Before leaving for the US he had appointed an executive to replace him, but whatever his merits, the son insisted he could not win with an invention that was without prospects. Again the executor opposed his wishes and said that since he deemed the deceased to have died while domiciled in England, the consultancy funding would be subject to heavy inheritance tax. Regardless, the son persisted in seeking the settlement on the basis that it was better to receive some cash than none at all. The executor responded by saying that 'his client' (as that was what he was, hat or no hat) would approach the purchasing company independently and continue to supply advice alone. This threat induced the son to ask his father's ex-wife (who had remained with the firm on its sale) whether it had any substance. She replied that there could be little threat since consultations had been very few, and no doubt her directors would be pleased to be quit of their obligation at a price.

The additional tactic was delay. The executor's client was still in place to receive the sail trainer's income stream – indefinitely, it seemed, if agreement was not reached. For the executor it was equally advantageous. As he wrote letters to himself and others, plus elaborate resumes of where matters stood, he was able to pay himself accordingly as he sat on the funds of the estate. But where, you may ask, were the solicitors to the administration during all this? Miss Joan Rubinstein, it seemed, was never in the office. She had delegated her obligations to a subordinate who could never act (beyond gentle chiding) until Mr Buckley Sharp had assembled the estate's assets. Complaints from the son (at one meeting, vociferous) were disregarded. Similarly, letters from solicitors acting for sisters of the deceased went unheeded; they were even told that their nephew was the cause of all the delay and one of them misguidedly took him to task for this.

As a crowning indignity he was obliged to ask Mr Buckley Sharp for funds to pay his solicitor and meet his own expenses. The inconvenience was not his least concern. In pre-motorway days travelling from Bristol in a small car took a long time. The shop and the attending bailiffs required his presence. Only in retrospect can the risible fiction of the executor's 'scrupulous' accounting be appreciated. Keep account of your expenses (meeting the companion at the airport, etc), said the executor, and you will be reimbursed on completion of the administration. The son, however, was asked to make an offer for his father's clothes in store. It was obvious that a realistic price was expected. There were no other males mentioned in the will, so any use his aunts might have made of them is doubtful. Obediently he sent a cheque and did in fact receive them.

Mr Buckley Sharp held all the cards, and how a specialist lawyer might have forced each issue at every point is conjecture. He had the ear of the Foundation as he was placed to assess the value of the sail trainer and consultancy asset, so he could dictate all terms and delays. His co-executor, too, was compliant and quite prepared to accept that the son was the problem. The son and his solicitor were at a loss to see any remedy. The executor made much of the surviving partner's allegation that the deceased had promised him in the event of his death his two controlling shares, although no written proof of this was ever produced. Stalemate continued and each party waited to see whether the other would blink first. Understandably, the long-widowed aunt was annoyed at the lack of progress. Coincidentally her neighbour's daughter was the surviving partner's wife (an added irony was that the son in happier times had introduced them), and she claimed to the aunt that the nephew was obstructing her brother's wishes. Under this pressure the nephew was made to feel very guilty indeed. Conversely, guilt and embarrassment at unexpected good fortune ebbed slowly from his mind: it was plain that the administration was malign and he must do his best to confront it.

Appropriate sentiments; but 'negotiations' (and of these there should have been none, as it was his father who had held the controlling share) were halted. But benefits were not stopped for the partner: the 'consultancy' continued and as another year passed he received payment from the diminishing fund. Probably, with hindsight, this would have been the moment for the son to apply to the court for 'letters of administration' which might have forced the executors to put extraneous matters aside and wind up the estate. (However, according to some authorities this process has a poor history of results in English law, is difficult to obtain, and is little used.) Alternatively, some suggested that his young solicitor was not a specialist in these matters and he should appoint another. The son, however, was never in sufficient funds to pay the quite reasonable accounts outstanding to his solicitor. And the farcical element was that he was obliged to ask the executor (wearing another of his conflicting 'hats') to approach Zurich for money to pay him. (In fact both of them: Mr Buckley Sharp was not providing that service for nothing!)

Additionally, with any thought towards a change of solicitor lay the problem of the cost of familiarisation of matters and events with a new advisor. Perambulations were well into their third year as the files piled ever higher under the weight of letters (distributed all round) that the executor wrote to himself. Recourse to a firm offering the terms of 'no remedy, no fee' was not an option in law as that process had not yet been accepted. So the novice, so to speak, stayed in the saddle for the ride.

The 'ride' concerned the stalemate. What amounted to blackmail for things to proceed was the necessity to trust the surviving partner (the executor's protégé) and transfer the controlling share. Though the son buckled under this pressure it was plain that Zurich had given Mr Buckley Sharp their support: they would not distribute the Foundation without his agreement. Erroneously, as it proved, the son had consented to resolution of the 'problem' of his father's house-sale proceeds lying in a non-residency account, by agreeing (generously) that the money should be distributed among the beneficiaries of the English estate. The son's agreement was circulated through a memorandum of understanding.

The Foundation also accepted the executor's assertion that the son had conceded the conduct of negotiations on the sail-trainer royalties to the executor. Would the situation and outcome have been different with a more expert lawyer to contest this? (At this moment it is reported that the whitest heat of legal mind is charging £1,000 an hour.)

Finally the son conceded the transfer of the controlling share, subject to a written understanding that regular progress reports and accounts would be provided. He and his solicitor now awaited finalisation of the estate.

However, apart from an interminable series of further delays designed to add to costs, events themselves were astounding. Ever meticulous to legal form when it served as a masquerade, Mr Buckley Sharp now gorged upon a banquet conjured by his sleight-of-hand out of a mere morsel of detail. This concerned the pricing of the two shares for transfer to his client, the surviving partner. He was now able to embark upon a year's correspondence in the form of instructions to nominees in letterbox-brass-plate companies. It was always helpful that he had created these companies himself.

The Cayman Islands, Bahamas, Swiss Foundation, the surviving partner's Swiss Foundation, the other executor and the son's hapless solicitor were all in the wretched loop. And all for what? To learn, after much prompting, that the two transferred shares were valued at £26 each. With this record, needless to say, promised accounts were never produced. The son's angry voice demanding them at a meeting with the other executor's subordinate (as solicitors to the estate) produced no result. The executor lamely accepted Mr Buckley Sharp's explanation that he was constantly requesting them in writing, so far without result!

At this point it is difficult to believe that worse could follow, but with their main object achieved the adversaries exploited their gains further. Probably to cover his back which was now somewhat exposed to the other executor, Mr Buckley Sharp disclosed that the sail-trainer company had admitted two new British investors. As to the dilution of the son's capital in the company, Mr Buckley Sharp and his client were not in the least concerned as they said the new people would ensure the project's success.

The son and his solicitor were told that the advent of these new men came at a price. They insisted that the salaried accountant (ostensibly a drain on the royalty revenue) be dismissed immediately. A greater shock followed: the 'new investors' were not investing any of their own money. Their 'investment' was to be provided from the royalty revenue stream each year and when this was exhausted this 'loan' from the sail-trainer company would fall due! It was apparent that the promise to pay back the loan was a fiction and that the new 'investors' had dismissed the executive to increase the sum available for their plunder.

Confronted with these events, and with a reinforced sense of horror that the architect of this fraud was administering the estate (which had seen no progress on the pretext of these alleged sail-trainer problems), son and solicitor now pathetically took stock. Their first assessment was that the English house-sale proceeds, despite the fact that the purchase and resale proceeds belonged to the son as sole nominated Foundation beneficiary, had been generously offered to the English estate without quibble. Contravention of non-residency rules was simply a penalty matter for the Revenue. Nonetheless, confirmation of these facts was sought from counsel, whose opinion was firmly in support to the extent that should restitution be denied, "proceedings for its recovery should be instituted immediately."

Accordingly, the son's solicitor advised the executor of this result, requested return of the money and withdrew consent to the memorandum of understanding. Mr Buckley Sharp refused, and when threatened with litigation wrote to the other executor stating that unless he received a writ he refused to believe in the reality of these proceedings. Correspondence was handed to the son by the executor to distance the executor from these events, and Mr Buckley Sharp called the son's bluff: he knew he did not have the means to sue.

A greater prize for the executor was that now the onus for delay could be laid at the son's door. The royalties had been plundered (and at legal costs to the son) and the executors could continue to empty the estate by charging these 'costs'. The aunts, incurring legal costs themselves without result, were of course informed that their nephew was to blame.

Casting about in desperation to take some initiative to force matters, the son was not heartened to read another letter supplied by the executor. This was from Mr Buckley Sharp and stated that the son would not (without his agreement) receive money from the Foundation until the house-sale proceeds in dispute were agreed and an accommodation reached with the deceased's companion.

The problem of the deceased's companion now loomed. Other than minor window-dressing to help cloak the real reasons employed (and described) to the executor's advantage, the matter was initiated by the son. This would not have been the case had the executor opted for the deceased's domicile in the US. The companion's conviction that (the rigours of the test notwithstanding) he had achieved a new domicile of choice would have cast the lady in a different light. The executors had not so chosen, so they could point to opposition to their view as a delay not of their making. However, with events unfolding as they had done, and the administration now into its fourth year, the son could not now avoid the fact that the executor was untrustworthy. It was obvious that there were advantages to the executor in immediately opting for UK domicile involving repatriation of the Foundation's funds. He had disclosed the value of the fund to the UK Revenue and if he could secure the agreement of those concerned to release it the money would pass through the executor's own hands for final settlement.

The lady, perhaps in her late thirties, as already related was very distressed on her return. Although it struck the son that her family seemed prosperous, he accepted without question her word that she was destitute. Furthermore, and much in her favour, she had been devoted to his father and her loss plainly went beyond mercenary considerations. As the months rolled by and intractable issues forever asserted themselves the son became increasingly concerned for her situation, all the more so as she most plausibly stated that his father had intended to make provision for her but had not done so before his sudden death. This determined the son to find a modest capital sum for her, and to this end he offered some land adjoining the house, the proceeds from which (the house) he had already offered the estate.

The land adjoining his father's house, as with the building, was held in the son's name (no doubt an unsatisfactory method of avoiding non-residency regulations). Before emigrating, his father had mentioned that he had retained the land for him. The generosity of this gesture at the time escaped the slow-witted son, but he was soon made aware of the implications by the executor. Having been complicit enough when his client was alive, he now made much of this contravention of the regulations.

An almost humorous incident now occurred, unrelated to the administration. Lodged with the executor, the Land Registry title could not be found. The pomposity of the law firm's apologies was in ironic contrast to the depredations so often wrought by that profession on the public. The matter was remedied (a new land certificate was issued), and the next event was a meeting of all parties in Zurich, at which the executor depicted the situation with elaborate obfuscation while the Foundation officials confined themselves to occasional interventions. These were made largely to remind those present that they were not behoven to any other country's tax administration.

Suddenly these proceedings were enlivened by the entrance of a vociferous man, who waved his arms as he strode about. Even allowing for the fact that English was perhaps his second language after German, he was most repetitive. He continued his rant until the audience began to examine their shoes with embarrassment. But not the passive and uncomprehending individual hitherto bemused by most matters described! No! He was transfixed by this diatribe. The man was saying that the lady companion should, as per written instructions to the Foundation, receive £40,000 forthwith.

It was plain that the speaker was receiving little attention and even less sympathy. The son was shocked and outraged. It was now his turn for theatricals. Leaping to his feet, he expressed his horror at this reluctance to comply with the deceased's wishes and insisted that the lady be paid immediately. There was then an interval and the audience retired for lunch, whereupon his solicitor tactfully explained that only the written statutes concerning named beneficiaries could take effect. The son learned further that officials in the 'foundation' (or 'trust') business often received similar letters, which explained their lack of enthusiasm. Some indeed might even be received from earlier companions of testators not yet deceased. Despite this explanation this stance was unacceptable to him and he insisted the lady be paid. The officials thereupon passed the matter to the control of the executor, with the proviso that they be indemnified against any adverse consequences of this decision.

On learning of the amount reserved for the companion, in comparison to their expectations from the English estate, his aunts were dismayed. The son was now handsomely cast as the villain, especially since he had, owing to obvious fraud with the sail trainer, withdrawn his offer to place the proceeds of the sale of his property in the estate to their benefit. Unaware of the letter produced at the meeting, the lady's champion was disappointed with her behaviour and politely asked her why she had chosen this underhand course of action. Her solicitors, she replied, *had advised her* not to disclose to him her initiative to obtain money in Zurich. After that, naturally, the son no longer saw the need to assist her and did not offer her the proceeds of the land sale.

That money disappeared soon enough into the maw of the bailiffs, shop and flats. The administration was completely stalled. The royalties had vanished, at vast cost to the son and, as a consequence, also to his aunts. But for the executors the honey-pot of their 'costs' remained in their keeping. (Neither interim nor final accounts were ever offered.) They camped on their position that the son had caused the delay – and, horror! – had even threatened proceedings. A letter alluding to the son's lack of means to sue from the executor, (handed to him by the other executor), stated (referring to money from the Foundation), 'and he will not be able to touch that until [the father's companion] is out of the way'. With a fifth year in progress the lady had married but her claim remained in place.

Momentarily in funds from the land sale, he offered £500 to his solicitor for work outstanding. This was accepted and he took the files to Bristol. Travelling costs to London would be saved and, he reasoned, legal fees would be less, thus offsetting the awful cost of the familiarisation fee with a new solicitor. Appointing a new one, he advised the man the obvious strategy was to obtain a statutory declaration from his late father's companion stating that the father had, in her opinion, obtained a new 'domicile of choice'. The chances of its acceptance by the Estate Duty Office were not high, but the shocking record of the administration made it imperative that it be attempted. This too despite the fact that her cooperation was in effect bought.

The new solicitor, however, chose to put this plan to one side and persisted in threatening the executors and bombarding them with letters to which they replied with interest and pleasure. These rivaled Mr Buckley Sharp's in length, but this man's talent went further. He excelled at subjecting his client to long lectures on a situation which of course never developed. His quarry squinted into the light at the darkened silhouette of the large man who sat framed in the window. Ever-gullible and inclined to accept that things were being done for his own good, the son nonetheless finally remarked that the situation was straight out of *Bleak House*. The solicitor replied, "Dickens was invariably hard on the profession."

With the files aging and ever-thickening this solicitor felt obliged to try something else. He resolved to batter upon the doors of the Foundation, just as he had done fruitlessly with the executors. The worthies in Zurich simply *had* to understand his point of view, forget their provisions and release the funds. Together they travelled by train, as the solicitor thought flying 'unnatural'. The Foundation officials reappraised their visitor with the situation that the files had described over and over again. Before sending them away empty-handed they took the son aside: "Mr Waddington, we are the people to help you – you should talk to us." He was unimpressed. They had obliged the executor in every manner possible. To keep their systems in place they blenched at any threat of litigation and demanded indemnities against every move. Such indemnities are said not to be worth the paper they are written on, but require the resources of King Midas to defeat them.

And now they told him that the controlling share transfer and the scrip for the incorporation of the new 'investors' was 'not a good delivery'. Well! They had dealt with Mr Buckley Sharp!

Returned to their hotel, his solicitor still felt he could get the better of the Foundation and amazed his client by asking that he appoint him as trustee. Somehow, he managed to refuse. This did not deter the man from appointing a new counsel to invent another trust vehicle to receive the Foundation's assets. Why could he not understand that they held both the padlock and key?

The answer to that question soon became plain. His client as a generator of fees was a prize to be held at all costs. Any new uninvited contortions in trust-deed drafting would only meet with short shrift in Zurich. Converting the expectations of a beneficiary held under strict statutes into back-to-back loans stood no chance, and the solicitor had been told as much.

Nevertheless, the client saw counsel in smart modern chambers and received an impressive opinion featuring words and phrases such as 'settlor', 'donor', 'in anticipation', 'selling in advance of' and 'loan in reversion'. On leaving, the client noticed the chambers had a clear view of the opposite side of the street. On crossing, he was accosted by a man selling a book on the history of Venice. The author's name was unusual and displayed on the book's jacket. It was the counsel he had just met. The man was keeping station where he could be seen to work diligently. This was all legitimate, yet bizarre and disconcerting.

Exasperation was now a permanent feature of the son's life. There was no movement, so the solicitor deemed it the right moment to present a bill for £5,000. The severe inflation of the late seventies was still some way off and this was an outrageous sum. The man had dealt in a small way with the son's divorce but only to the decree nisi stage, and had arranged a public planning appeal for a building application (this, like the marriage, also failed.) Earlier bills too had been met without quibble. He refused to pay, so a court hearing was arranged for a 'defendant in person'.

Appearing before the 'master' was in no way an ordeal: everyone was most courteous. His initial declaration was dismissed for 'prolixity', but this was largely a matter of legal form and was soon remedied. With the (sometimes comforting!) laws' delays the procedure was moving towards 'discovery' of documents when suddenly the solicitor withdrew his action. He proposed that he keep the building plot, the deeds to which (another valuable lesson!) were unfortunately in his possession. The land was worth less than the bill and possible costs, so the proposal was accepted. The files were of course to be returned to him forthwith.

Domestic disruption meant a return to London. Here in his impecunious state he was kindly given free lodging by his long-standing business friend in Marylebone in return for regularly chauffeuring her to her country house. A free agent once more rather than just a generator of fees, he approached his agenda almost with relish. Much as it was a lost cause, the sail-trainer fraud could not be ignored as it was related to the misfeasance regarding the Foundation and the English estate. Mrs Malnick, the companion, too must be pursued. Understandably, she had her price for providing a declaration. To her pursuer this was crucial, as without it Zurich would not release the fund. As to the acceptability to the Estate Duty Office (no matter how many times he heard that a person's domicile was a matter of fact and nothing but fact), this could in terms of natural justice never be separated from the motives and behaviour of those who decided the question. His first solicitor, as a result of dealings with Mr Buckley Sharp, advised him never to accept the executors' decision that his father had retained his domicile of origin in England.

That decision too held the son in another vice. Being at the time a UK resident for tax purposes, he now was obliged to pay tax, as calculated by Mr Buckley Sharp, on the earlier gift from his father, because the gift was made while the donor was still alive (known as *inter vivos*) and he had died before the end of the seven-year period following which tax would no longer have been payable. The son's ability to pay this tax now lay in the gift of Mr Buckley Sharp. The Foundation would not move without his say-so. Equally, he controlled the English estate – and enjoyed the moral high ground in explanations to the aunts of their nephew's behaviour in withdrawing his earlier offer!

With a divorce settlement looming at any time of his wife's choosing, and the tax due to the Estate Duty Office, as notified by the executor, the financial situation was not promising. In letters to that office he explained why he could not pay and made submissions and presented evidence concerning his own view regarding the question of domicile. Mrs Malnick's testimony was central to his case, and after a rather prolonged negotiation of terms she at last offered her 'declaration'. She was duly paid by the Foundation, so one of the two 'conditions' was now removed. The other concerned the executors' view (which the son had initially endorsed then declined) that his father's house-sale proceeds, although owned by the Foundation, should be distributed in the terms of the English will.

As to this last, Mr Buckley Sharp was making no move to finalise the estate, confident (after two further years) that the son would not commence proceedings. Therefore everything, no matter how seemingly futile, should be attempted to make the executor finalise the estate. Visiting the police's Fraud Squad, he was told brusquely that they did not touch wills. He then approached the executor's professional body in accountancy and was amazed to learn that they only investigated complaints of failure to answer letters. Aghast, he replied that the problem was quite the reverse: the man both wrote to and answered himself at length, and, dissatisfied with his restricted audience, even sent copies far and wide. Affronted by these aspersions cast upon his professional body, the official snapped that any remedy was a legal matter and stalked off.

Next stop: the offices of the Law Society. Result: a self-aggrandising, patronising leaflet so rudimentary that it would lead anyone with concrete, well-documented grievances to despair. No process was offered by the profession's policing body for neutral and binding arbitration to bring dignity to the law. And further disappointment with the Law Society followed.

He travelled to Bristol to collect his files as agreed by the Court, but his ex-solicitor was absent. Unconcerned, he stated his business to the partner, who thought it best to telephone his principal for confirmation. Delivery was refused. Nonplussed, the visitor began to rage and shout, whereupon the partner, a small timorous person, took fright and called the police, who escorted him from the building. There was no reason for the refusal: the land transfer had long since been completed as per agreement. His ex-solicitor held the position of Her Majesty's Commissioner for Taxes! The ejected visitor wondered if unfolding events would ever lose their capacity to amaze.

Surely, now he thought, the Law Society would show some teeth. He sent a letter, then another, and another. Eventually a reply of one line was received advising that the solicitor had been instructed to release the files. Another trip to collect them (and the delay had been considerable); so a further letter to the Law Society asking did they consider that the complainant should be satisfied with that and that alone? Another delay, and another one-line response advising that the solicitor had been 'cautioned'. (Some years later the man left overnight for Australia, under a cloud.)

Truth being stranger than fiction, he took the files back to his first solicitor, this being the only course available. Six years on from his father's death, first there was no money to appoint a new one; second, no money to commence proceedings; third, the Foundation by its statutes was immune from action; fourth, this solicitor was familiar with events from the outset, and that might be helpful.

Together they agreed once again 'to instruct Counsel to advise'. (Was anything else possible?) The long accumulation of issues meant that consultations would be protracted and involve the solicitor's time in addition to counsel's fee. As legal protocol demanded that the client be accompanied for interview by counsel, his solicitor provided a young student clerk in his stead, to minimise costs. Travelling thither, this indelicate and forthright youth informed the prospective litigant that his firm only undertook litigation "as a favour to clients," adding that "We are a conveyancing practice." Of the case he himself knew nothing.

This reaffirmation of a fact of which he had been well aware was depressing enough, but was as nothing compared to the onslaught awaiting him. What need had counsel to be so witheringly rude? He was simply asking him what best could be made of a bad job which, too, was far from being of the supplicant's own making. (One reason for gratuitous arrogance, if displayed, is that the solicitor, not the client, is directly liable for counsel's bill.) Further to his contemptuous dismissal of the case, the man slammed his fist down on another stack of files for effect, shouting, "This case here is a hundred years old!" (Thought the son, "And long may you make it pay!") Retreating, the son reflected that, at least as far as he could remember, not even Dickens's characters had been witness to such a scene.

At the end of this road yet again, he paid his solicitor and collected the files. Opening one, at the last entry he found a caricature of himself saying "Blah, blah, blah." Sitting in at the interview, as obliged by the rules, the clerk had at least found some employment.

It was now plainer than ever that the offices of the law would not assist unless he had more money to throw at them. He had already shown, by attending the interview with a clerk, that he lacked money. Yet there were still answers to questions to be sought even if the answers could offer no remedy. For example what did the accountant think who had been dismissed as a precondition to the entry of the 'new investors'? He phoned him and he said he would "dig out some papers" and meet him at a prearranged spot on the way to another appointment. The moment arrived and he drew up in his car with wife and children. Getting out, he shouted, "It's hell in that car … I can't find any papers; and anyway, what did I get out of it?" No doubt angry at her husband's treatment, his wife had persuaded him not to co-operate.

Earlier the son, though fearful of the cost, had sought the help of a prominent world-wide firm of accountants, asking: could the executor and the Caribbean companies be forced to account? The surviving partner? The 'new investors'? Was their 'loan' repayable? In due course he received their reply: Yes, the loan was repayable. For the rest, the tone of the letter seemed sympathetic but evasive, intending to convey that the cost of closing the stable door after the horse had bolted would be beyond him. Despite the time spent, the sympathetic investigator did not charge for this advice.

The son obtained the London address of one new investor and phoned him. The man declined to talk beyond confirming he was an investor (and therefore had received money as a loan repayable at a specified termination).

He then visited his father's surviving partner for explanations in general and received just a non-committal reply. Shortly thereafter the partner left permanently to live in the Caribbean.

Demanding accountability from the solicitors to the estate (the executrix's subordinate), at their premises, the son received one particularly contemptible response. He remarked that after almost two years even the two transferred controlling shares had not been paid for (which confirmed the Foundation's view of a suspicious action). Nevertheless, ever confident of his own safety, Mr Buckley Sharp read out a letter from the partner (his client), which declared, "I said I would pay but I didn't say when." The solicitor stated that this was "a matter for Mr Buckley Sharp" (under his three 'hats'), and did not comment further.

Following this meeting the son requested and was given an interview with this solicitor for the executor who (for his own reasons), handed the son what he may have considered compromising correspondence. In doing so he remarked, "Well, if Mr Buckley Sharp has done anything wrong ..."

The Foundation, concerned that they were holding share certificates for companies that they believed were valuable, sent the son information received from the West Indies. Following these leads further he learnt that the Cayman Islands government had withdrawn the practicing certificates for these companies in their jurisdiction. They had warned the Foundation that they would do so if their fees were not paid. The Royal Trust Company of Canada in the Bahamas similarly resigned as trustees.

Somehow, the Foundation obtained accounts at last and sent them to the son. Acting on advice, he took them to yet another solicitor for appraisal. By coincidence this firm was one floor below that of the executor in Gray's Inn. Unable to read accounts, he waited just a few minutes for the verdict: "Mr

Waddington, these companies have been milked." "What do I owe you?" "Nothing."

Considering regulation in the Caribbean to be somewhat lax, he visited the West Indies High Commission. Their advice was to write to everyone concerned and if he did not receive satisfactory answers within six months, "contact us again." This presented an interminable prospect: he did not have the investigative resources of the BBC! And in any case, to what purpose? The royalty money had gone.

He telephoned Mr Buckley Sharp to obtain his re-confirmation that the 'loan' to the new investors was 'repayable' as stated by the earlier advice obtained. The executor was absent so his son took the call and agreed that it was.

Reflecting on this exchange, it certainly seemed that these people were experts in 'due legal form'. Allowing for the unlikely possibility that they were unaware of what would transpire, their consciences were untroubled by any renewed prospect of the complainant incurring further expense chasing money that had vanished. This was a moment to recall once more that on his father's death the son had insisted that the sail-trainer venture be abandoned.

Without making a substantiated allegation on the matter, the executor's actions concerning a particular asset of the estate were questionable. The deceased's valuable harbourfront cottage was in a location so sought after that the very few properties adjacent seldom came on the market. The executor's duty was to seek an independent valuation and be prepared for a prudent delay for the circulation of details before considering the offers. The property was sold with undue haste. At an early executors' meeting Mr Buckley Sharp said, "We need to get money in and we've only had one offer so we've taken it. As a non-resident the deceased should not have owned the property."

It was tiny and repurchased to assist his ex-wife, who was always in financial difficulty. Five years had passed and the son questioned the agents. Unsurprisingly, they did not take kindly to his assertion that they had sold the cottage (albeit on instructions) too quickly and for too little. So he approached the owner and asked if he would allow access for a retrospective valuation. The owner agreed on condition that he receive in return a current written valuation. The son readily agreed and arrangements were made for the visit. Shortly before the agreed date he received a letter from the owner withdrawing the offer.

Estate accounts were not provided to the son, who was beneficiary to 60 percent of the English will. Whether his aunts, beneficiaries to the residue, fared better he does not know. Given that their nephew was successfully framed as the problem, he was not in a position to ask them. The son received no payment from the executors to fund his separate representation. An approximate value of the estate in March 1969: Proceeds of house: say £60,000. Cottage: sold for £11,000 (worth far more). Stored furniture sold, share holdings and other assets: unknown.

Finally the son telephoned Mr Buckley Sharp, seeking answers to obvious queries. A secretary consulted her employer, returned to the phone and said, "Mr Buckley Sharp says there is no more money in the estate to answer questions." As an executor, together with the other executor as solicitor to the estate, both were required by law to account for their own costs and the distribution of assets. The son had been unrepresented by a solicitor for a long period, and had he been represented no doubt some strange figures would have emerged. But he had been effectively seen off by the dishonesty of one executor and the laxity of the other. Following long years of embroilment, how was he to appoint another?

The telephone call had brought matters to a conclusion. Not only had he received nothing from the estate, but his royalty entitlement was also taken. It had also cost him incalculable sums to be so deprived, and the executor with supreme contempt had left it to his secretary to ring down the curtain finally in 1976.

Three years earlier he had been forced to cease trading at his shop. He just literally ran out of money to support it. His accountant advised the voluntary liquidation of the limited-liability company and arranged a meeting of creditors. Only two attended. They had done well over a long period as they, unlike their rivals, had held their nerve, continued to supply and taken good profits on their own terms. They shook his hand and left.

But the shop lease, as is usual, was not protected by a company incorporated with limited liability. Should he fail to dispose of the lease, his liability for rent could continue indefinitely. Owing to the high rates and restricted traffic flow the property company was unable to attract further tenants for indeed any of the five units in the parade, and following his closure failed to sign a permanent lessee for more than 30 years. Such a ridiculous situation poses questions. Even a huge property company must seek revenue for its investors from a parade of five shop units. Could it be that, favoured by the City Corporation for extensive shop and office developments, they in return refrained from pressure on rating policy?

Difficult negotiations now followed in an attempt to be released from his obligation. Finally, it was not too difficult to prove that he was not worth 'powder and shot'. His property was still under development for flats, and to make matters more complicated was held in common and equal shares with his wife. Following two further quarterly payments, settlement was accepted.

Heavy physical work on the old dilapidated houses was both opiate and balm after long months of jousting with bailiffs. Their money, of course, ran out long before they had their first tenants. Luckily the old properties contained lead piping and copper, which they sold for scrap. Scavenging in the skips outside other building sites too sustained their enterprises. Replaced floorboards were often still in good condition and they knocked out the nails, straightened them, and used them again too.

These were times well before tenancy reform. Since the advent of universal suffrage in the 19th century it was electorally unsafe for even Right-wing parties to ignore an always-large part of the population who insisted on the people's 'right to be housed'. Despite great efforts, centrally-funded local government could never build enough houses to satisfy demand for rental. Private-sector provision in addition was therefore essential, and such lettings were in huge demand.

Electorally, no government could allow plain supply and demand to control this market, and as with the lettings of government-funded council houses they had to insist on security of tenure, and – here was the greatest difficulty – at a controlled price. Property could not be developed for letting economically at this rent-tribunal-fixed rent. A further anomaly was that any older house as a prospect for re-development could only (if it was sold at all) be sold at a fraction of its real value if it contained a rent-controlled 'sitting tenant'. Worse still, property owners preferred to retain rather than develop these houses, knowing full well that tenants (despite any avowal to the contrary) would go to the rent tribunal. As a result, predictably the supply of houses for re-development almost dried up. This, and this only, finally persuaded the Iron Lady, the Prime Minister, that new (and only new) lettings should be freely negotiated at the market price. Then, cleverly (and to be even-handed about it), she 'gave' council tenants the right to buy their rented houses at favourable rates. Politically this was most dexterous as it showed she was not favouring the rich over the poor.

Government-controlled rents in London had, many years before rents were released, led to serious and serial violence. Led by a notorious specialist in the art, criminal gangs were employed full-time to intimidate tenants and collect inflated rents from them. Yet, finally putting the worst offender behind bars, the government thereafter did nothing as there were no votes in it until at long last the Iron Lady gave it her attention. As a manifestation of the abuses that can attend a controlled market, yet another offence became prevalent: with criminal intent, a house would be bought with often an aged and infirm sitting tenant and allowed suddenly to suffer accelerated dilapidation. The roof might leak (tiles deliberately removed), or through more direct intimidation the tenant would leave and the purchaser now had vacant possession of a house worth perhaps four times what he had paid for it.

Authority now countered all this with a typically 'catch-all' bad grace. It hit the law-abiding – those who simply hoped for possession at some stage, knowing that this was reflected in the price they paid. But to deal with the miscreants, the measures imposed invited similar practices from ill-intentioned tenants in return.

Unfortunately the son and his wife encountered some experts at this, a middle-aged couple with a child, who continually visited them, pleading to become tenants, after discovering that they were engaged in creating a flat. Giving in to the pressure, they accepted them. No sooner were they installed than they set off to the council, citing a small area of damp which the owners were happy to rectify. As a child was involved they succeeded in getting a 'condemned occupation order'. But would they leave? Not a hope! Such people knew full well of the endless backlog in the courts to secure their eviction. As the flat was condemned, they now paid no rent. Worse, there was even a traffic in such situations, to the profit of the tenants involved. Meaning that the landlord might find a new set of disreputable people in occupation, the incumbents having sold their occupancy to them for cash.

Remonstration could result in threats of violence. One had to wait for a court order requiring bailiffs to effect the eviction. Equally, from the side of council authority there was the threat of (commercial) violence. Even if the 'tenant' was enjoying an unrealistic rent occasioning loss to the owner, the occupant could still make an order to effect repairs. To no avail could the landlord plead poverty. The council was empowered to send contractors for repairs, put a lien on the property and charge 12.5 percent; and still the tenant would remain with a protected rent. Needless to say, mortgages to purchase a house with a sitting tenant were unobtainable unless one was imposed by the council as described. These had the effect of destroying the very thing they attempted to protect, and eventually a free market was the result.

Yet more advantage enhanced the heyday of the sitting tenant. They were entitled to refuse any alternative accommodation their landlord might find them. Infirm as she was and into her nineties, another of their tenants turned down all alternative offers. Should the sitting tenant be younger, however, with such a low rent he or she could save to own a house, taking good care not to buy one subject to the same restrictions.

Such was the distortion wrought by this housing legislation that its worst manifestation was as grotesque as it was inevitable. Many property owners, fearing an imposed uneconomic rent, opted to keep their houses vacant. Squatters then forced entry. Court action for eviction took so long that named parties could change on the order and the replacing squatters were therefore unanswerable – which no doubt they thought reasonable, having paid cash to their predecessors to move in! This lunacy naturally gave rise to even further distortions. Some landlords sought to make the best of a bad situation and accepted tacitly that their property was occupied. A 'settled' squatter, they reasoned, had an interest in keeping their property secure.

Councils themselves were the worst offenders, although they replied that central government kept them short of housing funds. Terraces of houses in their ownership fell to occupation by squatters. An acquaintance sub-let her squat on a prime riverside location in London for years, and accumulated enough money to buy a coffee farm in Brazil. The legacy of such abuses persisted long after the legislation changed. In a recent instance a long-term squatter was given ownership of a valuable house in an action contested by the council. This body had simply failed to re-take possession although legislation was in place for it to do so. Therefore not only had the man (an Australian) enjoyed free housing for 20 years, he pocketed almost a quarter of a million pounds funded partly by ratepayers. One London council's employees' behaviour went beyond the merely negligent. People had been on their housing list for years, only to be told that nothing was available. Eventually it was discovered that staff had been placing their own tenants in vacant flats and keeping the rents.

Dear Great-Grandson, those of tender age will see in all this a Right-wing portrayal and remark that housing resources are finite and compensating redress and restriction are necessary, et cetera. In this vein, a piquant example of the Right exploiting the situation is so notorious it has entered folklore. A London council leader, at some disadvantage as her electorate mainly was (and still is) housed by the council and therefore as is general votes left, remedied the situation by favouring her supporters who sought tenancies. As this titled lady had the resources and land of one of the wealthiest families in England, she was able for many years, first, to deny all knowledge and then, after exposure, to avoid the consequences. It took the persistence of a left-wing newspaper over many years to finally bring her to book.

Somehow, if only instinctively, the son felt, there must be more to life than all this difficulty. 'Instinctively' for, as one of life's innocents, he thought little ahead as to the consequences. The mantra 'plan the work and work the plan' dictates that desired events be foreseen. The son's habitual diversion from difficulty was entirely event-driven.

And so, dear Great-Grandson, conscious at last that any pleasure to be had in life was passing by, some, it was now thought, might be found on the sea. A new venture now presented itself in the form of a sailing boat. *Lady Rita* was a 36-foot ketch built in 1936 of pitch-pine on oak frames. The participants in this venture were 'bohemians' who might or might not possess artistic talent but what they all shared, even unknowingly, was an insistence on personal freedom. Some Bohemians would be Anarchists if they could get organised to be disorganised.

Her new owners discovered that she had an interesting history. Under a bunk, among rusting tools they discovered a commemorative plaque citing *Lady Rita's* participation in the evacuation of troops from Dunkirk in 1940. Possibly because *Rita* had been owned in the Irish Republic, which was neutral in the war, her owners had no interest in *Rita's* distinction, otherwise the plaque would surely have been displayed. At any rate, in 1970 nostalgia over the success of the evacuation was not yet widespread. The 'yacht' (somehow never so described: it was not just *Rita*; rather that impecunious bohemians can never be 'yachtsmen') cost him and his friend, Hywell Price, £1000 each. Bought at anchor in Conway, North Wales, she was in much need of attention. But it seemed they had got a lot of boat for little money. Far, far, from his mind was the old adage that the best two days in the ownership of a boat are the day you buy it and the day you sell it.

They sailed it to Bristol to fit out. As was agreed, he would pay for the fitting materials and his partner, a skilled sailor, would do the work required. This was not unreasonable as his partner had no money while he had no knowledge. But sweet reason did not enter into it. His partner felt his stock of knowledge was without price and resented that he did not own the boat outright. And this the more so as it was plain the son had merely 'come into money' and other than that had no evident merit. Dignity in the matter prevailed of course, and these sentiments went unspoken, but honesty prefers that they should not go unwritten.

There was a further, more practical inconvenience. His partner was a ladies' man. Many of that tribe despise men who are not. Convinced that the conquest of women is men's principal interest, they regard those reticent in this pursuit as inferior. At best their observations are patronising, thus inferring one's lack of ability. The consequences for *Lady Rita* were grave. The chap would turn up mid-afternoon, seemingly for rest and relaxation. And so it continued. One could not go in search of him: as tryst followed tryst, he might be anywhere.

Money, then time ran out as June, the month with the fewest gales, was approaching and *Rita's* seaworthiness remained questionable. The son thad arranged a 'charter' with acquaintances to be met in Gibraltar at the end of that month. The money they paid was to make a sailing sojourn feasible, or so went the theory. Well, they would need to be Bohemians like themselves: the yacht's accommodation had never been touched. Above deck, eventually some advance was achieved, but after too much delay. They replaced the rusted standing rigging against the risk of mast collapse. The decks were re-canvassed so that the heads of those below might keep dry (although their feet would not, from the bilges as the yacht heeled). The ingots of pig-iron acting as ballast were cleaned and redistributed in the bilges and (prudently) a powerful new bilge pump fitted. The engine was serviced, and that terminated the efforts of three months.

Rita had not been slipped for examination but simply sold afloat 'as-is'. The only indication of her soundness was that, at rest at least, she took little water. Yet when under way with her hull stressed under sail a plank could start and cause a leak. All such risks were blissfully unknown to the novice, especially as on principle his partner imparted little information. Ever cautious for the safety of his person, the son's experience stretched to dinghy-sailing within swimming distance of land. So, ignorant of the ocean's hazards, he called a halt, closed his cheque book and called his partner's bluff.

Foolhardy indeed, and his partner, a proud man, was not about to buckle and remonstrate in the face of provocation. So they set off with an old plywood dinghy with unmatched oars of unequal length to serve as a liferaft. The safety vests were non-inflatable, being of the old kapok-filled type. There were no distress rockets, but they did have some old, untried flares. They had no radio or barometer, but possessed an electronic depth-sounder. Worryingly (though for the novice only with hindsight), they had no generator to charge a failed battery – essential for an engine restart. In this situation perhaps he thought subconsciously that they could just get out and push! (One particular horror was that the voltage regulator gave no indication as to whether the engine's battery was charging or not.) Altogether it was "Yes, we have no bananas", but without the jolly tune.

The son was reassured, as he had heard of his partner's experience. He knew they had no sextant, nor any log-line to trail for measuring the distance covered, but to him these were just objects, said to be of use if one had them. His captain's last adventure had resulted in mishap. Having built with an associate a 26-foot plywood sloop they had set off for the West Indies and en route stopped at the Azores, anchored and gone ashore. On returning, strong winds had arisen, the yacht had dragged its anchor and was pounding the bottom. Once aboard they swung the crank of the petrol engine to make for deeper water, whereupon the yacht erupted in flames and burnt out to the waterline. Their explanation was that the pounding on the bottom had fractured the inlet pipe to the carburettor and a spark had done the rest. The British Consulate treated them well, providing new passports, National Insurance cards, the necessities of life and assistance back to England.

With three others as crewing passengers to help with the expenses until they arrived at Portugal, they set off. The plan was to turn east into the English Channel, provision at Newlyn, and then cross to Brest. At Land's End, in bright sunlight a fierce offshore gale struck – so strong that they came as close inshore as they dared. The old wire-and-pulley wheel-to-rudder system was too slow in response to hold the bow into the eye of the wind, and the captain gave an impressive display of his competence with the emergency tiller. Wedged tight against the pushpit, he was obliterated by each successive and solid wave from the view of those huddled in the cockpit. *Rita*, it seemed, was yet another lady he could bend to his will.

It was as well that the gale was not onshore. With experience the novice learnt that *Lady Rita* had no hope of clawing herself from a lee shore into the teeth of a gale. A Conway Cruising Club member had warned that Rita was 'tender'. Her builder, renowned for his safe and leisurely cruising yachts, seemed with *Rita* to have built a one-off, an exception and one that would sail faster. At 36 feet and with a 10 foot 6 inch beam, there was no scope for sufficient turn in the bilge. ('Turn' gives added volume to the hull and so adds buoyancy. Buoyancy provides enhanced flotation, which is stabilised by ballast or depth and weight in the keel. Of a piece with this slimness was the shallowness of her draught, at only 4 foot 6 inches.) To compound these limitations *Rita* was over-rigged, her mainmast being too far forward, and so should have been balanced by a gaff rig. Instead, in 1936 she had been fitted with a new powerful Bermuda rig. She could not 'stiffen' to carry it in a gale, and when pressed, could not beat off a lee shore. Pretty at anchor, she flattered to deceive and was unsafe.

Leaving Brest, the captain soon gave further evidence of his skill. To avoid the Bay of Biscay of frightening renown, they sailed west for three days and nights and then turned southeast on a course for Cape Finisterre, on the northwest corner of Spain. Whatever his faults, the man was meticulous in his watch for lights, upon which grief or safety depended. Rightly distrusting his company, he went without sleep to be certain of their position. This being a basic essential, it was plain that the rest of his seafaring had been done on a shoestring and many a maiden's prayer.

Risk and the resulting trepidation enhanced the pleasure and subdued relief at getting ashore. At each port they celebrated, soon emptying their pockets and giving them to understand why working seafarers are obliged to put to sea again. At Lisbon the last of their companions left as planned, and captain and partner were left together. *Rita* was not modern, and needed at the very least one competent crew member. To the son's surprise his generally unruffled captain expressed concern that he was with someone so inexperienced. Disheartening though this was, they set sail. Off Portugal, known for big seas, and alone at the helm while the captain slept, the novice was seized with fear. Speeding down the slope of the long rollers, he could not believe that on reaching the trough *Rita* would lift and climb the next. "Hywell! Hywell! We're going under!" Hywell appeared. "Don't worry: if that's happening I'll be the first into the dinghy!" (Helmsman glancing astern): "Hywell! The dinghy's gone!"

Bohemians so dislike convention that it is a matter of self-respect to disregard rules. To the novice it did seem inappropriate to tow a dinghy in the Atlantic, but deferring to the captain he had said nothing. The dinghy had filled in the big sea and the weight had broken the towrope. Had it not parted, a cleat and plank might have ripped from the deck, giving the captain a wet time below.

Cape St. Vincent, off Portugal's south coast, is a busy spot where shipping converges before dispersing. In the darkness the crew had difficulty with the rules of the road. 'Green to green, red to red: perfect safety, go ahead', runs the parable in *Reed's Almanac*. An old cargo boat was on a seemingly parallel course, so all was in order. But then it drew nearer and the novice lost his nerve. He felt the big ship's course was converging (as well it might if its intention was to pass astern of the yacht, the rule thereby remaining in place). Foolishly, he swung the yacht to starboard and so presented to the ship his port (red) side light. In haste, the steamer turned to avoid cutting the yacht in two, switching to a starboard course, thereby matching his red light with her own. This records the event but not the commotion. The old coal-burning steamer heeling, throwing a foaming wake, horn bellowing, engine thumping, then swept the unhappy yacht with searchlights and continued on. All this roused the captain from his slumbers and he appeared, then returned below without a word.

Arrived at Gibraltar, they were an all-too-obvious target for suspicion as smugglers. Unpainted for years and streaked with rust, the picture was completed with a circle of motor-tyres for fenders. The 'charter lady' duly arrived, while her husband was expected later. Perhaps she was unable to make comparisons, and this being her first charter, was too bewildered to remonstrate. Sportingly consenting to a sail, on returning she retrieved her large rigid suitcase freely floating among the floorboards, which became dislodged whenever the yacht heeled. At least one full-length ball gown was seen when the contents were hung along the boom to dry. Reluctantly she agreed to sail with them to Marbella, as the town is a noted resort.

They all now enjoyed a magnificent stroke of luck, for the showpiece marina of Jose Banus was receiving its finishing touches and awaited its opening by none other than General Franco himself. Like cheeky urchins they sneaked in. Perhaps they were thought a hazard to health, as they were left entirely alone. There was no other yacht to be seen. Moored to a pristine white stone quay bordered with lawns and palms, they had the swimming pool all to themselves for two blissful weeks. The only cloud was the daily altercation their charter had with horse-and-carriage drivers who she accused of cruelly treating their charges. (It was true that the horses' were so thin their ribs showed, but perhaps they just needed worming.) She would rush into the road and seize the bridles, shouting at the bewildered driver in English.

Any possible repercussions from this behaviour were curtailed by another turn of events. One morning they awoke to footsteps on the deck and found the police in the process of towing them sway to a secluded part of the marina without as much as a by-your-leave. Not being entirely without dignity they felt unloved and so sauntered on up the coast to Malaga and its luscious desert wine. The 'charter' returned home. She was rather 'county', and oddly was reputedly a hard rider known to ruin horses' mouths.

Malaga was memorable for a phenomenon that most would not forget. In old film of Australia a whole hillside from a distance may be seen to move. Only on drawing closer is it plain that shoulder-to-shoulder, obscuring the ground beneath, the hill seethes with rabbits. In Malaga it was fish. They rode in on the backs of fish with scarcely water between each, stretching from harbour wall to harbour wall. Uniformly black and ten inches in length, they were not sardines, the only other prolific fish in the infertile Mediterranean. Prompting the memory is the recollection that any notion impecunious yachtsmen may have of staving off hunger with rod and line are best forgotten in those waters.

Alicante, they heard, had that great rarity, a municipally-owned slipway. Their anxiety was acute, for *Rita* had not had her bottom examined, and perhaps not even for an eternity before they had bought her. The Mediterranean has the dreaded teredo worm, which bores big holes in wood. The town's quay accommodating yachts was run by an amiable Englishman who presided over the queue of boats waiting to be slipped. Given the ancient arrangements (and remembering this was before hydraulic mobile cranes that pluck yachts from the water like so many toys), the dozen or so boats were enduring a demoralising wait. The two fantasised that they heard the teredo playing cards as a diversion from turning their yacht into gruyère cheese.

Manifesting itself yet again from 15 years earlier was bank fraud. Letters of credit for specified sums at designated dates our innocent had arranged with his British bank were invariably at least a week late, and entailed being turned away empty handed from Spanish banks. They were proving as adept as the French, turning his money to profit on the international exchange. What made this crime so odiously venal was that the sums were pathetically small. They were simply pooled with larger sums for the benefit of the bank. His partner had no money, and as a chain-smoker he might dispense with food, but nicotine – never.

A boat and crew tied up in such circumstances is an unedifying spectacle, but more misery yet was about to lend enchantment. They began to notice that their agreed turn in the slip queue never eventuated. They complained to the affable English quaymaster, but the response was always "Next time, next time." At last the son (the pecuniary concern being his own) taxed an interloper with the matter, suspecting bribery. For the son bribery was quite outside his background and experience, just storybook myth like blackmail and ransom. But now, as a reality, it could join with shoplifting and professional fraud. (The queue-jumper admitted he had "done what was necessary"'.)

Nothing could be done about this, for who in general will admit to bribery? The quaymaster knew they were without money to cross his palm, and for further humiliation they were obliged to leave *Rita* with him for the winter. The son returned to England to work on the old houses, and his partner to dispense further his charm and favours.

The following year the captain wanted to sell his share, so the novice was obliged to ask *Rita* to reveal her secrets (she of course knew full well he could not sail.) He knew only that she was sluggish and capricious by turn, like the Mediterranean itself. So, after a fashion they struggled and straggled about, but always with at least one crew. *Rita* was determined never to trust herself with him alone. They visited the Balearic Islands without any embarrassing incident, then traversed the Gulf of Lyon and moored in the river at Agde. *Rita* was watched by a boatyard on shore, reputed to stand no nonsense, and they returned to England.

Rita, on moorings, had of course that *je ne sais quoi* that had induced even his experienced ex-partner to part with his every penny. Swept by the glistening river, this effigy to romance and stateliness deserved better than another encounter with mere mortals. With the new season the yardsman rowed them out and en route delicately disturbed their reverie. Rats, he said had been aboard, but he had got rid of them. Rats had swum from shore and climbed the anchor chain (picture them in the moonlight.) Stoically, they cleaned the vessel (no longer a goddess) but luckily found no poisoned bodies, as rats seek water after being poisoned. Then they set sail for Corsica. There was a hint of breeze as the river's current set them on, and they were cheerful, being with *Rita* happier with too little wind than too much. New to them was fog – not dense – with visibility at a constant 50 yards. And so they ghosted along, content that fog at least denotes settled weather.

With fog the river mouth was now out of sight, so he hurried below for a chart to set a course. He knew there was one depicting their route, but then made the discovery that rats had eaten the entire centre of that particular one. *Rita* had dozens of others, none of which were touched. Luckily the Corsican coast and their point of departure had not been devoured, so a compass course could be set. They drifted onwards with the sails just filling and no more. He regretted that his schooling had not been stricter, governed as it had been by an unusual captain. Here they were in fog with neither radar reflector nor foghorn, and so a hazard to themselves and others.

Of *Lady Rita's* many charts? Thereby hangs a tale. Following the evacuation of Dunkirk *Rita* was requisitioned for the war by the British government. It was not unusual for small yachts to be used in support of resistance groups in occupied territories. *Rita* was known to have escaped in haste from the Channel Islands, leaving some of her gear behind (perhaps thereby compromising resistants). On learning of this from Rita's builders, it was not lost on her latest owner that those brave enough to assist resistants would be the last to fear her lack of stability (although no doubt they had a well-cut cotton sail now replaced with a heavy terylene tent). In wartime the least of their worries would have been the seaworthiness of their craft.

But now she was steadiness itself! Onward they ambled, making at least two knots, he hoped, as the Gulf of Lyon has an almost two-knot current sweeping north and east along the coast. The light air abeam from the southwest, he knew, was pushing *Rita* towards the coast as her leeway seemed to run at one unit in ten over the ground. The correct procedure was to go about and tack south. But this was in the opposite direction to their destination. Anxious about the navigational guesswork this would entail, the nervous novice instead held to his course, mesmerized by hope.

Night came, but the breeze did not increase. Had it done so, with better speed they might have pointed higher and corrected southwards away from the coast. Soon there was a new sound as the wind changed note to a higher key near the shore – a continual sighing without pause, as with a sea-shell pressed to ear. There was hardly time to drop anchor. Just as feared: the Rhone delta! Where, as usual with great deltas, the ever-changing shoals give no indication of the shore, which with deltas may be well over the horizon. With no tide in the Mediterranean to lift one free, it is no place to run aground. Much chastened, and with a clear dawn, they crept away next day.

Corsica, being mountainous, is difficult to miss, so did not present the problems just encountered. Accordingly, they scored a direct hit on Napoleon's birthplace, Ajaccio. As with Napoleon, so with Corsica: the French attitude to the two is ambiguous. The former: hero or tyrant? The latter: jewel of the nation or liability? For a century, and ongoing, Corsicans have excelled at squeezing Paris for subsidies under the threat of increased violence by the 'independantists'. Corsicans do not deny that their culture and history embraced kidnap with violence for ransom. Known in French as *L'Isle de Beauté*, it well merits this description with its ever-changing colours, with blends so intense in hue they resemble enamels overlain with diamonds of splintering light.

In contrast to this parade of colour is the deep and cold shade of the Calanque, a long and vertically-sided sound leading to Bonifaccio. Perched on the cliff were the barracks of the French Foreign Legion. From over 200 feet the legionnaires' massed evening song floated down into the huge canyon and dominated nature itself.

Given the general locality, a trip to the Riviera was logical, so they sailed north. Logical too was the need to verify the lights. But befitting its reputation, the Riviera is a blaze of light. Up and down the coast they sailed, with the novice conscious that his ex-partner would have identified their destination without effort. Exasperated, he put in finally at the nearest port to hand. Morning came, plus man and dog along the quay. "Good morning" was returned in English (encouraging: one could make an inquiry). "Is this Nice?" (their destination). The reply came, "This is San Marino [Italy]. Nice is 60 miles to the west! Where have you come from?" "From England!"

Monte Carlo interposed itself twixt them and Nice. They would not be playing the tables, but the place (and Palace) were there and they were going in. And tied up. A tender powered towards them. "How much is it to stay?" "Nothing if you're out before dawn tomorrow." This was depressing: here was *Lady Rita*, sprucer by far than when purchased and with a proud history in which the denizens of that principality had decidedly not shared. The age had arrived when yachts were expected to be fat, similar, shiny white plastic, new and certainly safer.

After that snub they boycotted bourgeois Nice and sailed on to Cannes. Its old port looked attractive, so they tied up to a ring in the wall. Morning came with the gentle advice that the ring belonged to someone just temporarily absent and for which he had parted with £3,000. They moved on to Saint Tropez and managed to hide well enough. As is obvious, its continuing allure is owed to a recipe whose ingredients only the French can blend: starting with a simple fishing village, they dressed it with a festive air. Then their genius: how to make it permanent. The yeast must keep working. So it is forever a film set, with successive adept mayors to promote it as *the* place to be and be seen. A frisson of carnival pervades for which it is necessary to cram a cross-section of humanity into the place. But to admire and envy, one must see the showpiece of this pageant: the mega-yachts of the super-rich, arrayed in line stern-first to the little quay. Their male owners recline and display in an indolence worthy of lions in a zoo. Langorous beauties in sarongs feign independence through indifference. A dozen yards from the gangplanks, waiters stand in deferent attendance at permanently reserved tables.

The islands offshore made for a relaxing contrast, but then there is a troublesome sailing passage called La Ciotat. The route to the next port lies close inshore. Somehow the coastal configuration affects the wind in a bizarre fashion. Wind may continually and frustratingly change direction, but generally streams parallel to land and sea. Not at La Ciotat! There, vertically with the high cliffs, it funnels downwards with great pressure. The waves run to no pattern and the sea is siphoned up, then dumped in a crazy vertical chop. *Rita* was pressed into the sea almost to her deck and, alarmingly, would not answer the helm. Rocks were close by and it seemed that was their destination. But as time went on they found they were in less peril than it appeared: the current ran parallel to the shore and sent them through. They stopped at Grasse and Marseille before wintering again at Agde. Of exploration ashore there is nothing to relate. There might be money for a sack of potatoes, maybe not. They were stuck to their boat like poor Chinese to their sampan. But sailing in the sun was a recompense, although the new South African crew promptly left the boat at the next port.

The next season, at Agde, a boy of 17, of Vietnamese and French parentage, asked if he could crew and was readily accepted. He had just completed a sailing-dinghy course for open water well offshore in Brittany. Having heard of a courageous dinghy passage of over 400 miles between Norway and England, and hearing his recruit was of that persuasion, Rita's guardian was most impressed. So they set off.

Arriving at Porto Cervo in northern Sardinia, they found themselves alone. Prince Ali Khan's mansion was somewhere about, but not visible. This beautiful area, known as the Emerald Coast, was aptly named, and gazing into tranquil depths one might even doubt that the substance was water. The place was as-yet undeveloped and even a shop was said to lie at a daunting distance, so they lay at anchor wondering what to do next. At last they decided to sail to the nearest port, Rome, some 90 miles distant and bearing 90 degrees east.

Three days of this contemplation had seen the weather deteriorate: no wind but ever-lowering skies. 'He-who-must-be-obeyed', or as the French say, 'The sole master on board after God' was reluctant to set off, and insisted on two more days' delay. This brought no change. Had they a barometer they would have seen the glass was plummeting. Lacking Italian too, the transistor offered no forecast.

Disappointed in the delay, the inescapable inference from the boy's opinion was that his captain was over-cautious, and foolishly yielding, the latter agreed to sail. It was as if that very act decided the onslaught. Just clear of the harbour there was no hope of return. Striking from the north, though their course was due east, they would have to run south before it. But first they must drop the mainsail and mizzen, which meant turning into the wind. *Rita's* response was so violent that any thought of lying hove-to under bare poles was abandoned. The two sails were dropped but could not be stowed, and so gave too much windage. As the storm increased, so did Rita's speed.

Leaving the wheel to the young crewman, and with a line around his waist, the captain went forward on hands and knees to drop the jib. By good fortune he had heeded advice to acquire a storm jib, which is small and made with heavy fabric to avoid shredding. The sail changed, he crawled gingerly back to the cockpit. With centre-cockpit yachts this position is actually well aft of centre. In creeping by, he saw with alarm that the keel beneath was the first part of the boat to make contact with the water. They were planing like a surfboard! And furthermore, to survive they had better keep their speed as close as possible to that of each wave. Ideally, the crest must pass on ahead, but gradually, thereby lessening the force of the wave advancing from astern. Any thoughts that this procedure alone would save them were soon dismissed. The wind, increasing yet, and so their speed, was making the yacht unstable. *Rita's* ridiculously over-tall badly placed heavy wooden mast swung to and fro like a metronome, dragging her with it. Come what may, the boat must be slowed in her mad career. Going forward again, he reduced the jib to hardly more than the size of a door. Now came a new problem: the rudder responded too slowly to the wheel. The old-fashioned cable system, which carried slack in order not to lock up, could not respond in time to a new danger: rogue waves, not directly astern, but from the quarter.

These waves, resulting from slight shifts in the general wind direction, are superimposed on the main wave pattern. Though of less weight, they rush in on the quarter, with greater speed. Thus are yachts pooped by a breaking sea that comes inboard. The crewman, with his dinghy experience, offered to use the emergency tiller, and going aft slotted this six-foot bar on to the rudder. Wedged into the metal bars of the pushpit, it was as well that he could not see the spectacle behind. He had become the captain of the vessel and their fates.

The steering was now more positive, with no risk of yaw, but the wind increased and darkness fell. From the cockpit it seemed *Rita* was as likely to drop forward into a hole as to be swamped from astern. Accordingly, he volunteered to crawl forward again and drop the rest of the storm jib, hoping to reduce the speed, even by however little. The helmsman refused the offer, insisting that they maintain their speed. He pleaded, but still the young man refused.

Unable now to influence events, and rather than peer into the night to no purpose, he slumped to the cockpit floor, completely resigned: it was not a matter of whether they would die, only *when*. A planing boat or a surfboard is, barring mishap, stable, but *Rita* was rocking violently. Looking up, he was glad she had no masthead light to follow, making frightening arcs in the sky. Sooner or later she would broach, roll, fill, and founder.

In 30 hours the storm abated. The boy had brought them through. They had come to the Iolian Islands, 260 miles southeast. The first encountered was Alicudi, where they dropped anchor. Fervent prayers of thanks for their deliverance were now appropriate, but those in peril tend to pray during, not after a crisis. So, sullenly they rowed ashore, churlish for their fright, and clambered up the island's slopes to gorge on cactus pears.

The Straits of Messina, between Italy and Sicily, now seemed a logical destination, and Stromboli, with all its dramatic aspects, lay en route. In the 1950s the ice-matron Ingrid Bergman succumbed to her film director Rosselini thereupon or thereabouts, and promptly put the island on the map. That she had earlier played the saintly nun in 'The Song of Bernadette' was helpful too. One could say she was to Stromboli what Gracie Fields was perhaps less so to Capri. The steep slopes of this active volcano cast a forbidding wind shadow of flukey, shifting airs, and the water was so deep one might bump the island before an anchor held. Disappointed that they had not got to grips with its smouldering mysteries, they backtracked to visit the island of Filicudi. Approaching, they became intimidated by the splendour of the villas and felt they could not land and just stroll about. Snubbed already twice in their wanderings, they were not going to risk a third. So they stayed with *Lady Rita*, consoled that she enjoyed a title.

In the morning they resumed their journey to Messina. Or so they hoped. Another storm struck from the north, obliging them as before to run south. Incredulity that they could be in the same situation again so soon was at least now tempered by familiarity. They should, too, reach the Sicilian coast before nightfall. Yachts for safety beat in successive tacks into an onshore wind to reach greater security in open sea, but with *Rita* this was not an option and they drew comfort from the knowledge that land lay somewhere ahead. The storm set fair to be as bad as the last, and they would have run her up the beach as if she had wheels. It was well that the sea was calm that day at Dunkirk in 1940 or her soldier passengers would have sought other transport.

At last, thankfully, in summer daylight the coast hove in sight. In their predicament that was the first consideration. Their next was where were they? Their chart was only small-scale and showed only the big city of Palermo, which they hoped very much lay before them. Surfing closer, however, no city was discernible with its welcoming port but seemingly only a flat, straight shore. Palermo was, they realised, out of sight to the east and *Rita* would never cope with the beam-on rollers if they bore away eastwards. By instinct, even if imprudent, land appears as a prospect of safety for those in peril on the sea. In any case, with no choice, they came on.

Then, oh joy! What appeared as beach and breakers became a stone breakwater. Closer yet; a single mast visible within. A few minutes more: an entrance, and on the opposite wall a crowd of people. No surprise, for it was Friday evening, when Latins like to stroll and take the air. Nearer, something odd: these people were jumping up and down and gesticulating to the east. They had seen *Rita's* mast and size and were adamant she should make for Palermo. *Rita* knew differently. She drew only four foot six inches, and the height of the modern aluminium mast they had seen indicated a yacht which, although smaller, undoubtedly drew more water.

As Rita rushed to the entrance, the captain (he had reinstated himself) turned her beam-on to check her speed. Nothing else was possible, as the harbour was tiny. With that, a local would-be hero dived into the surf and struck out, plainly intending to get aboard and save them. A boathook to ward him off was not required, as *Rita* just slewed her bow inside the wall and regained way. As they swept in, anchor and chain went sharply over the side. The storm was rushing her still towards the harbour beach, but at last she checked, held, swung and settled without a single slap on her bottom. They all felt snug – not to say smug.

The next morning the weather had quietened, and as there were no shops handy they decided to sail to Palermo. The anchor, however, would not come up. They dived to free it, but in the storm-churned murk found chain that would not lift or was not their own. Gloom descended through the remaining Saturday and all of Sunday. On Monday, they knew, fishermen would come to take their boats out fishing to feed their families. Of course they would find in turn that they could not free their boats as *Rita* had fouled their moorings. There was time to contemplate the very worst of outcomes. How many boats had they fouled? Was there heavy harbour-floor communal chain to be lifted? Would cutting equipment be needed? And what of their own situation? They had no money; Britain was still outside the EU, and *Rita* was unregistered, so unprotected against writ.

Monday came, and three fishermen rowed to their boats. Peeping over the coaming, *Rita's* worthies watched as the men tried to lift their moorings. One by one they raised their gaze to the culprit. Sheepishly, her captain appeared to acknowledge their fault. Without a word the fishermen slipped into the water, and at the end of a long morning freed everything. With only gestures at their command, *Rita's* company expressed their gratitude. Smilingly, and with the eloquence reserved for their countrymen, the fishermen indicated that all sailors were behoven to help one another in difficulty.

At Palermo they marveled that such a sinister old town could be the abode of similar hearts to those they had just met. Perhaps, unlike small shopkeepers, poor fishermen were not under the burden of compulsory tribute. Inevitably the saying came to mind: 'Any actuary can tell you how many people will die next year, but a Sicilian actuary can give you their names and addresses.' A pleasant sail along the coast followed before turning right into the Straits of Messina. Regretting their lack of Classical education, they discovered they had joined company with the whirlpools of Charybdis and Scylla. Charybdis was quiet on this occasion and did not snatch and devour any sailors, though she did affect the helm. But *Rita* was unconcerned, as the current sets south and so together they sauntered on in the sun.

Leaving *Rita* in Catania for the winter, they looked forward to crossing to Malta in the spring. Once there, her enslaved owner made use of the excellent facilities to make her look beautiful. So she could again flatter to deceive. This took time, so they spent their leisure moments in part worrying about Colonel Gadaffi, who had deposed King Idris of Libya while the latter was on holiday in Greece. In four years from 1969 he had scarcely been out of the headlines for causing problems near and far. As Malta is not far from Libya, and with their intention to sail to Greece, the slightest possibility of being blown onto Libya was unenticing. All previous attempts at registration having failed, *Rita* tried again, outlining the risk to her person without consular protection. She was accepted almost by return of post.

A blissful sail to Greece followed, of the kind that more than compensates for every difficulty. What is known as a soldier's wind – just aft of the beam at a constant force – took them all the way. Rita had acquired a new, modern sail to compensate for her sad old sagging mainsail. This new genoa was much too powerful and she could not carry it above a constant Force 4.

Landfall at Zante offered a picturesque walled harbour bereft of any vessel. A man in late middle age appeared from nowhere, bringing fruit and flowers. To their shame the man through gesture indicated that these were gifts of welcome (as indeed they looked bewildered). It was chastening to reflect that they were so devoid of culture they had not learnt that the ancient tradition in Greece is to welcome strangers in this way. Sailing to the northern shore of the Gulf of Corinth, they planned to see Byron's house, which entailed passing up a reedy river. Here Byron had helped organise resistance against the Turks. Once again a courtly gentleman appeared and with sign language insisted that Rita's captain should accompany him on a tour of the village tavernas. A visit to the tiny port in the vicinity of Navarino followed, where in 1824 a combined British and French fleet had defeated the Turks. The passage through the Corinth Canal leads to the Aegean. This very old canal is mystifying. Deep-sided and cut through the isthmus as if with a ruler, it had been weathered to looking as natural in the landscape as the pyramids of Egypt. *Rita* then arranged to spend the winter alone on a secluded beach.

One might ask, "How did she get up there?" If fishermen could be persuaded, and at some risk, *Rita* could be hauled ashore like their own caique boats, and thus avoid a long trip to a proper yard, perhaps unaffordable. Such yards had cradles on bogeys running on railway lines to slip yachts with long dagger-type keels. The risk was that *Rita's* keel, although running her full length as with a fishing boat, was deeper than a caique's. If the contracted fishermen did not chock Rita stable and upright she might wobble and threaten to crash to the beach. On one occasion the men took fright and did not reappear for days.

The sheer antiquity of the slipping system was a delight. Greased, weighted baulks of timber were first placed in the water and a wooden floating cradle then drawn as far as possible under the boat's bow. A tractor or motor-winch would then drag boat and cradle forward until both sank on to the sunken, greased skids. The boat emerging with jerks, fits and starts, the system required that the greased baulks be hastily retrieved from the water and placed successively under the advancing vessel. In such manner did *Lady Rita* totter up the beach, as if approaching the bar for yet another port-and-lemon. The glory of all this lies in its antiquity, as the method dates from the Stone Age. Man's best friend, too, enters upon the scene: stray dogs appear, attracted by the smell of boiling sheep offal used to make tallow for greasing the skids.

Ashore at last, *Rita* was however not ideally placed for disputes over the price for returning her to the water. The Greeks do not have a western view of binding contracts: for them the cultivation of connection is all-important, and binding agreement secondary. The Greeks themselves know this. The expression 'Beware of Greeks bearing gifts' is their own. If the success of the Greek shipowners is at variance with this view, one must recollect how their fortunes were founded. Many seamen drowned from sinking ships fit only for scrap while their owners enjoyed too-negligible taxation, insurance and crewing costs.

Assuming the cloying pre-requisites of artificial friendship were followed (and not before those more adept had pushed in front of the re-launching queue), *Lady Rita* could return to the water. It was the time of the Colonels' putsch and with it their attempt to annex Cyprus to Greece. They held a plebiscite to confirm their legitimacy with a plain choice of 'Yes' or 'No' offered to the populace. In the island of Spetses the visitors saw the overwhelming majority of houses had 'Yes!' (in Greek, 'Ne!') posters in their windows.

Rita set off for the northern Aegean and her crew became aware that the political climate had changed. About to anchor close inshore at a small island, and with no other boats in sight, *Rita* attracted attention. Patriotism, it seemed, had inflamed the locals sufficiently to drive, brandishing guns, to greet her. She had not seen such hostility since Dunkirk and the Channel Islands. Frightened by these people crammed into the back of a lorry, *Rita* departed. The Turks had invaded from the mainland to support their compatriots, and war had broken out. Arriving at Kavalla, in the north, *Rita's* company marvelled at the fervor of the Greeks, shouting and waving from the tops of tanks as they raced to the frontier. They hoped to reclaim Istanbul as Constantinople, the ancient seat of their Church. It was well that peace broke out, as such was the muddle that on opening their ammunition boxes the Greeks found anything but that commodity.

Sailing on, they felt safe enough to take a glimpse of the Dardanelles and Gallipoli with their grim memories from 1915. Byron, despite his lameness, swam across the Dardanelles with its strong currents. Today the heavy through-traffic would make this feat impossible. Travelling on, an island appeared (much as they do). Generally lax in such matters, as they approached land they consulted the *Admiralty Pilot*. This indicated that the island belonged to the Turks (whereas almost all are Greek), and it was forbidden to land (given their frequent wars), even in times of peace. And so they tacked away, to return to the phoney diplomacy of the pirates who held in a vice-like grip a monopoly on the over-wintering arrangements. As to winter, even in summer the northern Aegean can be chilly and one must take woollies as a precaution.

Next year they sailed to Mykonos. The harbour is easy to run into when you're chased from the north by the Meltemi. This constant summer wind approaching Force 6 often lifts stones from the seaward side of the breakwater, sending them over the top to where they land on the decks of the sheltering yachts behind. The wind not so long ago was put to good use by a profusion of windmills. 'Tramping' ships brought wheat from the Ukraine on the northern shore of the Black Sea, to be ground for flour. The ships would then tramp off in a roving search of any other cargo and then return north for the next wheat season. Many bunkered en route at Aegean Island coaling stations like Kea before making for the Dardanelles.

Lady Rita's visit coincided with events that were relatively new. Mykonos had become a Mecca for those who only later would describe themselves as 'gay'. They had their own nudist beach and a regular Miss Mykonos contest. The winner ran a lap of honour through the village in silk shorts, a victor's sash and crown of flowers. Abashed at such competition, but only after several attempts, *Rita* managed to leave harbour into the teeth of the Meltemi. Her 'Ali Baba's tent' for a mainsail never made things easy but a new one was financially beyond reach.

Such limitations notwithstanding, they had begun to fancy themselves at maneuvering into small island-harbours without recourse to the engine. Backing the jib by hand, as in dinghy sailing, was quite within their compass. Long gone were the days when they would throw a line on berthing to someone on shore without having first attached their own end to the yacht. However, the eventual consequences of nonchalance are a near-certainty and humiliation was soon to follow.

After Mykonos they approached Tinos, and on arrival headed for its quay at a brisk pace. This was intended, as nothing looks sillier than dropping the sails too soon, leaving a yacht with no further impetus to reach the landing. Worse, having failed, the yacht might drift and sweep lines of small fishing boats tied to one another from their moorings. At least they'd never been guilty of that.

So with confidence they sped on until the captain signalled to drop the stern anchor. This done, it was just a matter of paying out the warp, dropping the sails and checking the line's run so the bow would arrive just short of the quay. Then from the bowsprit one would step elegantly ashore. But things did not go to plan. In mitigation, at least he knew instinctively what had happened. The ring that keeps the crossbar at right-angles to the flukes of the anchor had broken. Normally this bar would force a fluke into the sand, but instead the anchor folded into a flat object and skidded merrily across the bottom. Twelve tons of yacht was closing on the quay at trotting pace and there was nothing, it seemed, to prevent a calamity. Between them and the stone quay stretched a necklace of fishing boats. Sadly, the gaps in this necklace were large and they would pass easily between two boats. (The property of others plainly would not save them.) Only seconds remained before a splintering impact.

Rita reared from the water like a whale broaching to blow, then plunged back and stopped dead. They were saved – but how? Hastily dropping the bow anchor, they glanced sheepishly about. Then all was revealed. The connecting line between the two fishing boats sagged beneath the water's surface and mercifully had caught Rita's keel. The line had not been severed, as the boats had acted like buoys and absorbed the shock. They had upended skywards with the impact and *Rita's* weight on their line had dragged them under. Luckily, they had bobbed back up and were just afloat.

A throng of fishermen gathered on the quay some 40 yards off. However, as they could see their boats were safe their jeering tone denoted sarcasm rather than rage. "Hey, Captain! Captain," they yelled. The spectacle took him back some years to the drunken Saturday night crowd who had gathered outside his burning shop. Obligingly, his crew (it was not a moment for the captain to put in an appearance) got into *Rita's* dinghy, paddled over and bailed their boats dry. Oddly, while Mykonos is known for hedonism, Tinos is remarkable for penance. Once a year devout womenfolk crawl to the summit of the island on their knees – with blood in some evidence. Perhaps the yachtsmen had escaped serious punishment.

Lady Rita was discreet, so she did not keep a diary or ship's log (to confide in writing is to share with another.) Of fickle and feckless partners she had had her share: why else had she chosen to shroud much of her past in Irish mystery? That she chose with pride to wear her heart on her sleeve in part absolved her current owner from the shame of planning their divergent future. The planning soon turned into a dream. *Rita* let it be known that no one was suitable so they stayed away in droves. Perhaps being slightly older than her current suitor made her determined that together they should endure. Increasingly, the maintenance of her dignity was proving beyond his means. Unless someone turned up he could envisage a time when to stop the expense he must just give her away. Ruefully, he recalled a similar situation with the fish-and-chip shop. In desperation he approached her builders. They recalled her brave war history, now more than three decades distant, but indicated they were builders, not brokers.

That 'second greatest day in the ownership of a boat', it seemed, would never come. The animism of the situation was ever present: that the wooden vessel always in need of attention was not just a material object, but had a soul

But at last an admirer succumbed to temptation. And fittingly, not just anyone. Harry Butterworth Junior the Third, an American southern gentleman, had not just the name but a personality in lights. With poodles, cigar, toupé and an ouzo-imbibing entourage, he was not a person the Greeks could afford to ignore. Such a celebrity would raise *Rita's* profile too, so she could hardly object. With huge relief our protagonist banked the cheque.

Greece was subject to exchange control. Greeks could not take money out of the country without permission, and only then after payment of a large premium. As a foreigner he was exempt, and was issued with papers to permit withdrawal. Soon afterwards his wallet and papers were pick-pocketed. Neither the bank's receipt, police statement, nor sworn statutory declaration would persuade the bank to release the money. Eventually, a Greek bank employee phoned to say he would obtain release to England on payment of a commission to him of 11.5 percent, which he was forced to accept. The episode recalled the experience of a Greek friend in Greece who received an expensive false diagnosis for a costly operation for which (as was confirmed abroad), he had not the remotest need. The 'descent' of the Jews for verification is through their mothers; the Greeks behave as if the matter is out of their hands. To quieten any feeling of guilt they resort to myth. For Greeks, their mythical Gods (and therefore for them, real) are so much worse.

The alternative to the entrapments of the sea being plainly the land, he attempted simple reflections of its beauty in water-colour. As is well known, the arts 'explain life'. Fiction depicts life through imagination and is therefore a constructed lie. Unlike fiction, factual reportage follows events so cannot 'explain' life but only draw conclusions that often remain open to question. In contrast, through constructed character and events a worthy fictional novel explains life. The parallel in painting is demonstrated by Monet, where instead of reportage, light is the passing 'event'. Painting the same scene every 20 minutes, Monet showed that the scene was compromised and opened to different interpretations through light putting truth in question. So, as with the novel, a painting too is a construct of the imagination; a lie that hopes to offer a greater truth.

The novice, new to this problem, admired the discipline of Victorian ladies who, following the advice of Samuel Palmer, ensured that their water-colours were completed within two hours. With time ignored too as a factor, light's nemesis – shadow – as deployed by Palmer, models the scene in relief. Thus, as with fiction, the painting is an artificial construct, albeit one that may convey 'a greater truth'.

Crucially, as moving shadow obscures the subject from view, the painter is painting from memory.

The beginner painfully confronted this well-known problem but could not – would not – accept the discipline of the remedy which is painting (as outlined) from memory. Western art accepted it; Eastern art ignored it. So, joyfully following the sun as it lit each leaf – there stood the leaf to be painted! The result is flat if colourful, as to place shadow under each feature permanently lit is to emphasise that the problem of moving light and shadow has not been addressed. (And the attempt looks ridiculous.) In sum: there can be no compromise with shadow: it insists that you lie. The novice sold some with the years but his paintings could never be other than naive.

Away from these complexities is the simplicity of the land itself. With prodigious crops and contented animals there seems no limit to the bounty of the land. Some trees close by give it shelter, half-grown at 40 feet, crowd in and contest his every step. His passage through them, he accepts, is made to flatter his vanity. Tiring, a chance glimpse outward from the thick and dark conifers shows an eventual retreat is equal in distance to the point of eventual escape. Well, he must just take it slowly; that's all, and find some pleasure in his folly and reverie. How strange that these trees, so stately, yet vulnerable to man, can be felled in a trice. With the struggle they've had to lift themselves above grass, weed and scrub, which with effort they dominate, then banish, their fate should never be in question. Yet neither do they show each other mercy: lose the race upward to the light and you're dead, killed by your neighbour.

Well, God knows, he'd done his best for them. As a Johnny-come-lately from very far off; a supplier had sent him tree seedlings so small, they were of no use to hares and rabbits and so were eaten by his old friends – mice! Those deficient in the hail-fellow-well-met approach must suffer the consequences.

A tradesman with more work than he needs can indulge his spite with the added pleasure that he knows that, intentionally slighted, you won't be back. But once the dainty mouse-morsel trees stopped sulking they grew in confidence to face drought, fire and flood and the strength to fight each other. Oh! ... that's forgetting stock incursions and the wind itself – intent on leveling all before it.

It was beginning to seem that this excursion was a bad idea. The trees, at less than 20 years old, had not cleared themselves an understory. Unshed dead branches offered to poke him in the eye, and bending beneath each one was exhausting. Oh dear! Where man's vanity leads him! Remarkable: the handle of his hoe that planted these trees was still in good order; a man, too, had told him that hand-tools never wear out ... at last, a patch of light: he could sit down there and rest. Two defeated trees had fallen and opened the canopy. He propped his back against their heartless neighbour ... a good long rest would see him right. Soon, a stoat runs by, sees him, but pays no heed. This most purposeful of animals then runs up and down successive trees at astonishing speed like a roller-coaster. It is looking for nestlings. Time passes, and the light with it. Much, much later another stoat appears and bounds over the fallen trees and two stiffened limbs. Intent upon the hunt, it's not a scavenging rat – a stoat's 'stoatally' different.